Slade!

*The True Story of
the Notorious Badman*

Other books by Bob Scott

Tom Tobin and the Bloody Espinosa
Guts and Glorieta
Glory, Glory Glorieta
Blood at Sand Creek
Plain Enemies
Leander NcNelly, Texas Ranger
After the Alamo

Slade!
The True Story of
the Notorious Badman

BOB SCOTT

with a foreword by Chip Carlson

HIGH PLAINS PRESS

FIRST PRINTING

10 9 8 7 6 5 4 3 2 1

Cover art: Wood River Gallery

Library of Congress Cataloging-in-Publication Data

Scott, Robert
Slade! : the true story of the notorious badman / Bob Scott ;
with a foreword by Chip Carlson
p. cm.
Includes bibliographical references and index.
ISBN 0-931271-67-3 (hardcover, limited edition : alk. Paper)
ISBN 0-931271-68-1 (trade paperback : alk. paper)
1. Slade, Joseph Alfred, 1829-1864.
2. Outlaws--West (U.S.)--Biography.
3. Pony express. 4. Overland Stage Line--History.
5. Frontier and pioneer life--West (U.S.)
6. West (U.S.)--Biography. 7. Carlyle (Ill.)--Biography.
I. Title.
F593.S56S36   2003
978'.02'092--dc21
2003011432

HIGH PLAINS PRESS
539 CASSA ROAD
GLENDO, WY 82213

WWW.HIGHPLAINSPRESS.COM
ORDERS & CATALOGS: 1-800-552-7819

For Linda and Bob

who constantly encourage me.

CONTENTS

FOREWORD

A MONG THE legends and lore of the Old West's truly bad men, a few stand out – names, that when mentioned, immediately evoke thoughts of danger, perhaps, indeed, of evil itself. One of the pre-eminent ones is Jack Slade.

Considering that Slade's history dates to an era (he was born in 1831) when record-keeping was often hit-and-miss or non-existent, an attempt to verify episodes can be frustrating if not impossible. Yet Bob Scott has produced what is arguably the best single documented history of the colorful life of this infamous figure of the West.

Reading this account immediately impresses one with the enormous variety of Slade's adventures – and "adventures" is an appropriate term. A person will find it difficult to find words adequate to describe Slade's life; "colorful" is perhaps close, but still lacking.

Gaps in time where no information exists about Slade's doings add an element of mystery to accounts of his life.

He committed his first murder as a thirteen-year-old, in a vicious, bloody attack on a drifter. The episode revealed an explosive, uncontrollable temper. As he became older, his rage repeatedly got the better of him.

One of the remarkable things about Jack Slade was his toughness. After being shot and wounded – severely wounded – by Jules Bene and near death, he survived a long, difficult wagon ride to Kansas. The length of the journey and his horribly painful condition, in an era where medicine was more art than science, is hard to comprehend. Yet he miraculously recovered.

His pursuit of vengeance drove him to the savage, torturous killing of Bene. That episode in itself, which Scott has covered thoroughly, speaks of a brutality hardly known to twenty-first-century America.

As a bullwhacker and freighter and as a valued employee of the firm of Russell, Majors and Waddell (one of the principal companies that brought supplies to the expanding West), Slade showed an attitude of responsibility. He was, indeed, a dependable employee who could organize and carry out complicated projects. He was "the right man for the job" in more than one project.

And these were difficult times to be in America's vast frontier. Indian brigands had more than plunder on their minds when they attacked wagon trains. Often in violation of treaties guaranteeing no further encroachment on their territories, the white man's expeditions were destroying the Indians' hunting grounds and sacred lands and indeed their very way of life. The hate and violence that followed as certainly as night follows day was only natural.

Slade's effectiveness at establishing freighting posts along what were only primitive trails reflects an innate ability to develop and implement what were, in the era, complicated tasks. He had enormous ability to buck seemingly insurmountable odds. He fought off Indian and white attackers in episodes of incredible violence. His brutal killings of both, as punishment or retaliation for their own actions, was highly effective. Was he brutal and cruel? Unquestionably. Did he get the jobs done? Most certainly.

One is impressed with the striking contrasts in Jack Slade's temperament. In addition to his sense of responsibility as an employee, there seems to be little doubt that he was a devoted, conscientious, loving husband. On the other hand, his irascible disposition and fiery, uncontrollable temper – especially when in his cups – most certainly brought about his downfall.

It is only natural to this reader that a contrast between Slade's life and that of Tom Horn – with which I have a degree of familiarity – be made. There are similarities, in the sense that both were known to disappear for periods of time. There are gaps in each man's life for which there simply is no information as to his whereabouts or activities. They add a degree of mystery to our accounts of their lives.

Bob Scott's research has uncovered a world of facts about this enigmatic, heretofore little-known Western figure. He has, where possible, separated fact from legend with admirable investigation. This is a masterful job of weaving together the disparate threads of this enigmatic bad man of the Old West.

— Chip Carlson

Chip Carlson is the author of three books on the life and times of Tom Horn, the notorious stock detective of late nineteenth- and early twentieth-century Wyoming.

PREFACE

T HE JACK SLADE STORY has fascinated me since early childhood. Raised in Fort Collins, Colorado, and a frequent visitor to the Virginia Dale community as a child, I cannot remember a time when I wasn't interested in trying to find out more about Jack Slade. By the time I was an adult, it was clear to me that the Slade story had taken on "legend" status. It was also apparent that like so many other legends, there was an enormous amount of "poetic license" involved in much of what was written about Slade. After completing my fifth book on frontier America and the Civil War era, I decided to try to find out the real Jack Slade story.

That turned out to be considerably more difficult than I first imagined. Many books included tales about Slade, but almost none tried to cover his entire life. In addition, many of the books, newspaper stories, and other accounts carried fanciful and sometimes obvious distortions or downright untruths about Slade—including the interesting, but clearly not accurate, story about Slade authored by Mark Twain a hundred years earlier, perhaps never intended to be taken for the unenhanced truth. Reliable information was hard to find.

Fortunately, a few reservoirs of good information exist—places such as the Colorado Historical Society in Denver, the University of Nebraska Library in Lincoln, and the Larimer County Library in Fort Collins. Some of what appears to be the most factual information about Slade was found in the oldest records of early Colorado and Wyoming. Especially helpful was *History of Wyoming*, edited by I.S. Bartlett, and published in 1918, and the wonderful *History of Larimer County, Colorado*, written by L.L. Watrous for publication in 1911. Both of these books contain first-hand accounts of Slade's activities.

Also extremely helpful were several never-published manuscripts—hand-written documents we uncovered at various places. Among these was a six-page article written in 1934 by Don R. McMahill, who was attempting to compile an accurate history of Julesburg, Colorado, and a numbered manuscript found in the archives of the Western History Department at the Denver Public Library. There were a number of other hand-written notes, letters and documents from the Fort Collins Library's archives, many of them old efforts by local citizens to compile an accurate history of the area. A number of individuals were also extremely helpful in conducting research, including the staffs at the Denver, Fort Collins and Lincoln public libraries, and Barbara Dey at the Colorado Historical Society—all of whom exercised great patience while going out of their way to help us dig through old records to find information.

Even with the gems gleaned from these and other sources, there continued to be gaping holes in the story and lots of inconsistencies. It eventually became a situation in which I amassed all the books and articles and notes I could find from all sources, compared them to one another, and drew some hopefully logical conclusions about which were most likely to be true or close to true, and which were pure figments of the imagination and fancy. Over time I literally collected several large file drawers of articles and records on Slade. I also personally visited all the key geographical locations in the story—at least all of them which could be positively identified. Over a period of several years I produced what I believe to be a reasonably accurate and detailed story of the life of this incredible—and incredibly complicated—frontiersman.

You'll notice in the book that I try to specify when a story that is told cannot be verified, or when several varying accounts exist—something that is common. In spite of the difficulties in learning the truth about Jack Slade, I am confident that the vast majority of the information contained herein is accurate—or as accurate as possible under the circumstances. I am also confident that the story of Jack Slade is one you will find interesting.

TROUBLE STARTS EARLY

F ROM THE EARLIEST RECORD of his childhood, Jack Slade was both "different" and—to those with whom he disagreed—dangerous. Today, Jack most likely would have been labeled "dysfunctional," or perhaps incurably delinquent. Perhaps a crisis intervention center would have gotten involved early enough to have altered history. Of course those labels and treatments didn't exist in the middle of the nineteenth century.

It wasn't that Jack Slade came from a troubled family, at least not in the sense of a broken home or a family without love and support and the material things a boy needed. In fact, the Slades were seldom in need of anything. Jack's parents were the very cream of society in Carlyle, Illinois, in the 1820s and 30s— wealthy, politically powerful, respected, and civic-minded.

Jack's father was Charles W. Slade, one of Illinois' most prominent citizens. He was a United States Congressman and, prior to that, an Illinois state legislator. And even earlier, he had served as a United States marshal. Indeed, he was a very powerful man who knew the right people. In addition, Charles Slade was also wealthy, having earned his money through hard work and dedication. First he built a grist mill and made it the most successful business in his part of the state. Later, he almost single-handedly constructed a suspension bridge over the Kaskaskia River. That bridge not only permitted the town of Carlyle to spring up around his mill, but also permitted easy trade with neighboring towns in Indiana.[1] Mr. Slade remained deeply involved in town politics and was very influential in Carlyle. He acquired substantial property and his opinions and support were openly courted by the rich and powerful of Illinois.

Charles Slade married Mary Kain and between 1820 and 1834, five children were born to the union. Joseph Alfred "Jack" was the fourth, born January 22, 1831,[2] though some sources indicate that his birth year may have been in 1826 or 1833.

Mr. Slade ran his family as he did his business. There were assignments for everyone, and idleness was not acceptable. The Slade family was organized, doing exactly what needed to be done and doing it right. The townsfolk marveled at what a perfect family they were!

Unlike Mr. Slade, Jack's mother was quiet and unassuming. She tended to stay out of sight and spend her time doing the things a good wife did—raising the family and tending to the house. She was what the neighbors called a dutiful wife, and she was said to be a "perfect" mother.

Indeed, her children—two sons and two daughters besides Jack—were all proper children, respectful, studious, polite. But as for Jack—well, even Mrs. Slade couldn't do anything with him. To her closest friends she would wring her hands and confide that she simply could not control him.

By the time Jack started school, his father had become ill and passed away. He left his young family financially secure. In 1836 Mary married Elias S. Dennis.[3] That changed nothing in the boy's lifestyle. Jack of course had been raised a gentleman—his father and later his stepfather saw to that. Like his siblings, he knew the right things to say and do. When he was younger, Jack was a model of decorum, with perfect manners that impressed visitors. The boy was always well dressed and in need of nothing.

In addition to his looks and manners, he was quite bright. Jack was capable of getting straight "A's" in school, and sometimes did so when he was still quite small. However, by the time he was in sixth grade Jack had become a problem student. He often played hooky and rarely completed his assignments. Jack's frustrated teacher sent notes home with the other children. The notes resulted in trips to the woodshed, followed by stern lectures. They did no good.

His deteriorating grades were only one of his problems at school. Although smaller than most of his classmates, Jack was also much tougher, and he constantly picked fights to prove that point.

By the time he turned thirteen, Jack had a reputation as a bully and a troublemaker. He hung out with kids from the "other side of the tracks"—kids who had no family stability, no money, none of the finer things in life. With them, Jack became an undisputed leader, and the things he led them to were often not only dangerous or wrong, they were also illegal.

The summer of Jack's thirteenth year was when that first major event of Jack's life took place—the event that set the tone for the remainder of his life. It would turn out to be a dark omen about Jack's future.

Accounts of this incident have appeared in print for over one hundred years, some giving imaginative and poetic details and using what certainly must be created dialogue. From these sources we have compiled the following story knowing that, like much of what is known of Jack Slade, it may be more legendary than precise.

On a hot, muggy afternoon in August Jack and two other boys had gone down to the river as they often did. Skipping stones on the water or throwing them at frogs, the boys talked of swimming and fishing, about making slingshots, and of sneaking a smoke made from corn silk or tobacco stolen from their fathers.

All three of the boys were barefooted. The two bigger boys had no choice in this matter; each owned only a single pair of shoes, and those shoes were worn only for church or special occasions such as when Grandmother came to visit. The smallest of the three boys, Jack, owned several pairs of shoes, but he rarely wore them. He was barefooted not only because boys like to be barefooted, but probably also because the lack of shoes made a statement about his independence, and clearly separated Jack from his brothers and his family and the rest of the upper crust. Jack liked to thumb his nose at the high society lifestyle of his influential and snobbish parents.

On this particular afternoon all three of the teenagers were wearing faded overalls, the kind that had been repeatedly patched and handed down from older brothers. Two wore straw hats, but neither hat fit, and they slid down so far that the boys' ears stuck out like pump handles. The third boy was bareheaded. Altogether these three youngsters gave the appearance of normal small-town boys on any afternoon of the long, boring summer. In fact, had they been at school or in downtown Carlyle on a Saturday night, it would have been impossible for most folks to distinguish these boys from any of the other young teenagers of the time. Only a local resident familiar with everyone in town could have picked them out of the crowd.

Many citizens of Carlyle believed none of the three had much of a future. When the boys passed by, town gossips exchanged knowing glances. They clucked their tongues and shook their heads sadly, telling one another that these boys were destined for some dire fate.

Unfortunately, they were right.

The boys appeared not to notice the disapproval of the town folks. Or to care.

A few of the town wags reluctantly cut a little slack for the two bigger boys. After all, they were struggling against unending family shortages of food and clothing. Their father was a day laborer, often unable to find work. Their mother took in laundry and sometimes worked as a maid for the wealthier folks in an effort to simply put food on the table for her hungry family. Given their situation, it was understandable that the boys of this family wore ragged clothing and—since they came from the poor side of town—that they were hungry and poorly educated. Some townspeople were even forgiving of their bad attitudes since the boys had no way to learn good manners in one of those run-down homes across the tracks.

But the smallest of the three got no sympathy from the gossips. He was Jack Slade, the son of the dearly departed town father, and there simply was no excuse for his bad attitude.

On this particular hot afternoon the boys, Jack Slade and his two companions, by prearrangement had slipped away from routine chores around their houses and had met at their secret rendezvous site near the edge of town. Now some thirty minutes later, they were lying on the river bank. For a long time they lay silently, simply enjoying the fact that they had successfully slipped the bonds of parental supervision. They stared up at the clouds drifting lazily across the afternoon sky.

According to the few remaining notes on that day—notes written many years later—the boys' primary goal that day was to avoid doing any chores and to simply enjoy themselves down by the river. After several minutes staring at the sky one of the boys sat up and fumbled with a small paper bag. Then all three boys sat up. Each boy clumsily rolled a cigarette, lit it, and blew a great cloud of smoke into the summer afternoon. Then all three lay back contentedly once again, enjoying the quiet afternoon and pretending to enjoy the smoke.

Then a rustling sound in the underbrush startled the boys. All three bolted upright, wide-eyed, and tossed the incriminating cigarettes into the stream. A stranger emerged from the bushes and seemed quite as surprised to find the boys as they were to encounter a man none of them had ever before seen. The four stared silently at one another for several long seconds.

The stranger, a man whom history records only as "Mr. Gottlieb," was dressed in tattered clothing—rags, really—and had a dirty, matted beard. His hair, long and unwashed, flowed from beneath an oily hat, and he smelled of too many days without bathing. His shoes were scuffed, and the sole of one shoe flopped up and down as he walked.

Exactly what transpired over the next few minutes is not known. The hobo apparently tried to take advantage of the fact he had come upon the boys as they smoked. One of the boys later said that the stranger threatened to tell on the boys and laughed about how much trouble they were going to be in. Then, however, the stranger made them an offer. He said he would not tell their parents about the smoking if the boys would go into town and steal him some food. The hobo probably felt triumphant—and certain he was about to enjoy his first good meal in a while.

Unfortunately, he failed to realize who he was dealing with. The threats were more than Jack Slade could handle. The boy wasn't used to being bullied and wasn't about to take it—certainly not from this stranger. Jack's temper boiled up inside him, and he became determined not to let the hobo have his way.

Details of what happened next have always been sketchy. It appears that while the hobo was threatening the boys, Jack Slade quietly edged to his right until he was nearly behind the hobo. Slade bent down suddenly and his hand closed over a rock some six inches in diameter. Without pausing, the boy picked up the rock and again stood erect, concealing the stone behind his back.

At the appropriate moment, when the hobo's attention was on the other two boys, Slade leaped forward and brought the rock smashing down onto the stranger's head. When the stricken man fell backward, Slade was on him in a flash—using the rock as a hammer and smashing downward over and over again.[4]

If the hapless victim struggled at all, it was only briefly. The furious boy was unusually strong and determined—and he had become a whirling dervish in executing the attack. Over and over he smashed downward until at last the hobo lay completely still. Even then Slade apparently went on hitting for some time before finally stopping and sitting motionless on the man's chest.

The other boys later said they were stunned by the attack, but by the time either lifted his voice in protest it was far too late. Jack eventually stood up and instructed the other boys to help him roll the dead man into the river. When the boys meekly protested, Jack dismissed their fears. He assured them that if anyone happened to find the body, they'd think the victim had simply fallen from the railroad trestle. Besides, he said, no one was going to miss the dead man or come looking for him. Jack seemed absolutely certain that no one would ever know what had happened.

In fact, had Jack been alone he probably could have gotten by with the murder of this hobo. Of course, he was not alone. His nervous companions became the first of several major problems associated with the killing. The most obvious difficulty in terms of covering up the killing was that the other two boys were splattered with blood from the pounding. Slade himself was soaked with it. That much blood could hardly be explained as a nose bleed, and with no serious wound or other source for the blood, people most likely would have become suspicious anyway.[5] Perhaps Jack could have concocted a story about killing some animal had he been alone—but he was not alone.

And besides, in spite of his many bad habits, lying was not something that Jack did. He might avoid the truth for as long as possible, but when faced with an ultimatum, Jack was never in his life known to have lied—not as a child, and not as an adult. One thing he had learned from his father was that when it was time to take his medicine, a real man did so without protest.

But that speculation is academic anyway. The other two boys probably could not have kept the grisly secret under any circumstances. They apparently couldn't wait to get back to town and start talking about this shocking incident and to distance themselves from any responsibility. The bigger boys seemed to figure that the quicker they confessed all the details and separated themselves from Jack Slade, the less likely it was that they would get in trouble.

Pictured above is the Slade family home at Carlyle, Illinois, where Jack spent his boyhood years. From this home Jack was banished to Texas as a young teenager after killing a stranger. (Courtesy Western History Collection, Denver Public Library)

By the time Jack reached his own home at the far end of Carlyle that evening, the parents of the other boys were already on their way to summon the sheriff. When Jack was crawling through a bedroom window and changing his clothes to avoid detection, the town was already buzzing with rumors of the killing, and the sheriff was down at the river recovering the body. Jack and his family were only halfway through their dinner when the sheriff pounded on the door.

Little is known of the lengthy meeting that took place that evening at the family home. The meeting involved the sheriff, Jack Slade and his parents, and the parents of the other two boys. The other boys had already told everything they knew about the killing and repeated their stories for Jack's parents to hear. Jack may never even have been asked for his side of the story—and even if he was, he probably did not deny it.

After laying out all the facts, the sheriff is said to have strongly suggested to the parents of the poorer boys that they leave town that very night. The family agreed to do so and gratefully made a hasty exit. Long before sunrise the following morning Jack's two youthful companions were on the road to somewhere else and were never seen again around Carlyle.

That solved two-thirds of the problem—but dealing with the remaining third would be significantly more difficult for the sheriff. One simply couldn't order Jack's prominent family to make the young man vanish.

Eventually the sheriff pointed out that Jack was only thirteen and probably could not be sent to prison even if convicted of murder. On the other hand, he suggested that people of Carlyle would not be pleased to have a young killer wandering loose on their streets, even if the boy was the son of prominent citizens. The sheriff made it clear that the sooner Jack disappeared, the better it would be for everyone.

While never actually saying so, there was a broad implication that because of who Jack was—that is, because of the sterling reputation of his family—officials were inclined to permit some solution to the problem that avoided formal charges or a messy trial. The sheriff knew that no one was likely to miss the hobo, and, since he was not a resident of Carlyle, the hue and cry about his killing would be less intense. Locals would be more forgiving of Jack Slade than if only the poorer boys had been involved.

More importantly, the sheriff also realized that this could be a most convenient way for the town to rid itself of the trouble-making young Jack Slade before he got into more serious difficulty for which there was no easy solution. After a lengthy soliloquy, the lawman suggested that the most prudent course of action for all concerned might be to simply find somewhere else for Jack to live. Quickly. And the farther from Carlyle, the better for all concerned!

The sheriff later wrote that Jack's stepfather sat in silence, arms folded across his chest while the sheriff spoke. Then he rose and paced the floor for several seconds. Jack's mother sat in silence, wringing her hands, her eyes riveted to her husband's face. At last Jack's stepfather spoke. He told the sheriff that they had family living in Texas and believed they might be willing to take on the responsibility of looking after Jack. He would contact the Texas relatives right away. The sheriff said Texas sounded like a wonderful place for Jack to be.[6]

And so it was after an exchange of telegrams between Jack's parents and their Texas relatives, and only one full day after the killing of a stranger only tentatively identified as Mr. Gottlieb, Jack Slade and a battered suitcase of clothing were hastily loaded aboard the outbound stagecoach. Jack's mother wiped tears from her cheek and continued to wave long after the stage was no longer visible.

Arguably, that turned out to be the last time Jack would ever see his family. It would not, however, be the last time that his family or Illinois would hear about young Jack Slade.[7]

Notes on Chapter One

1. W.C. Collins, *The Hanging of Bad Jack Slade* (Denver: Golden Bell Press, 1963), 18.

2. O'Dell and Jessen, *An Ear in His Pocket: The Life of Jack Slade,* Loveland, CO: J.V. Publications, 1996), 2.

3. *Ibid.*

4. *The Hanging of Bad Jack Slade*, a book with considerable amounts of provable information, suggests that the hobo was killed when all three boys threw stones at him; it says one rock hurled by young Jack struck the victim on the head and killed him outright. In spite of the book's reputation for accuracy, this explanation seems unlikely and disagrees with known facts. It should also be noted that several reference books which cite no source for their information suggest this killing occurred seven years later when Jack was already an adult. This latter version of the killing almost certainly is in error.

5. The description of the killing of the stranger is based on historical accounts of the killing as recorded in the *History of Larimer County*, L.L. Watrous, (Courier Printing and Publishing, 1911), and on several other historical journals.

6. *The Hanging of Bad Jack Slade* says that Jack was sent to Saint Louis instead of Texas and says from that point there is confusion whether he went to live with relatives in Texas or California. However, the book notes that Texas was virtually lawless at this time and says it would have been logical for young Jack to have gone to the Lone Star State. Once again, this book is the only source of such information. The *History of Larimer County* and other evidence suggest that Slade went directly to his uncle's ranch somewhere in Texas.

7. While most writers agree that this murder occurred when Jack was thirteen and that it prompted him to leave Illinois, some sources have placed the incident much later. Dan L. Thrapp, *The Encyclopedia of Frontier Biography* (Arthur H. Clark Company, 1988), 1318, says the killing occurred in 1850 when Slade, then twenty-one, returned home from the Mexican–American War. No other source makes such a claim.

In addition to disagreeing with other sources researched for this story, the *Frontier Biography* account does not seem logical; such timing would not explain why the young Slade was suddenly sent from Illinois to the Texas farm of his uncle at the age of thirteen, nor does it seem possible that Slade could have escaped prosecution had he been twenty-one when the killing took place, in spite of the prominence of his family.

COMING OF AGE

V ERY LITTLE IS KNOWN about the next several years of Jack Slade's life, those so-called formative teen years. He apparently spent at least three or four years after the Illinois killing living with an uncle on a farm somewhere in central or western Texas.

In the 1830s Texas lay at the very edge of civilization. A few years after its war for independence and a few years before the Civil War, Texas was a rough and untamed frontier without sophistication, a place where men lived by their wits and their fists, and occasionally by their guns. It was, in fact, an area perfectly suited to the emerging personality of Jack Slade.

In the southern part of the state—in spite of one war already fought and another about to be—Texans still struggled against Mexicans for control of the land and the cattle that once were a part of Santa Ana's empire. The bloody and continuing battle led to near-anarchy. Men on both sides wore pistols strapped to their sides or carried rifles in scabbards hanging from their saddles. Ethnic hatred permeated the territory as white men snarled that the Mexican bandidos were stealing all their cattle, while the Mexican men complained about the crooked gringos. It was a land where a quick trigger and a willingness to shoot first often meant the difference between life and death.

West Texas was even less civilized than the southern part; here, Anglo settlers were locked in combat with Comanche,

Kiowa, Kiowa-Apache, Navajo, and Apache Indians, as well as the angry displaced Mexicans. The frontiersman who ventured into this untamed western wilderness to establish his homestead knew that the survival of his entire family might well rest in how well each of them handled a firearm.

It would be difficult to overstate the violent nature of life for these frontiersmen. The entire Texas frontier was a continuous battleground where violence and violent men were everywhere. One historian noted that, "The frontier was marked by lawlessness. ...The American carried his peculiar concept of justice with him as he traveled from one frontier line to the next. He took along his weapons and instruments with which to rob and murder. He toted well-established, useful techniques both to commit crime and to punish the criminal."[1]

In this atmosphere the men who managed to survive were those willing to face deprivation and hardship, literally fighting for their lives against great odds. Texas was a land where boys grew up quickly, lean and tough, and unafraid of anything.

It is not surprising that Jack Slade took to this lifestyle like a honey bee to nectar. With an apparent natural bent toward violence in spite of his monied background, young Jack was soon out-fighting, out-shooting, and out-drinking most men in the region. There are no known photographs of Jack Slade, but from descriptions of friends and acquaintances it is known that he became a barrel-chested, muscular, and somewhat swarthy young man. He was said at this time to have sharp features, jet black hair, and a perpetual frown.

But while Jack's physical appearance changed radically during his time in Texas, his attitude and behavior didn't change at all. Oh, there were times when he was gentle and thoughtful, and apparently he could be a loyal friend. Most of the time, however, he was angry and arrogant, and he still loved to pick a fight. Unfortunately for others, Jack had now also become as adept with a Bowie knife and a Patterson Colt revolver as he was with his fists.

By the time Jack turned sixteen years old he could hold his own with anyone, and under virtually any circumstances. It's not clear who taught him his pugilistic skills or where he practiced them—although given his surroundings one would suppose he had ample opportunity to learn. From the few accounts of his life during this "growing up" period it is apparent that well before leaving Texas Jack was well prepared to take care of himself. It is also apparent that he continued to be a bully. Since Jack in later years proved to be intolerant of "foreigners" it seems likely that his anti-Mexican and anti-Indian feelings were embedded during this time in intolerant Texas.

It is said that by the time he was sixteen, young Slade was the best pistol shot in the countryside. He often won spending money by entering and winning local shooting contests. He was able to hit the bull's-eye on a target at distances where other men could not even hit the target.

Given his personality it should not be surprising that Jack loved to show off his marksmanship to strangers. After enticing a stranger into a shooting contest, Slade would deliberately miss a shot or two and then place a bet that he could hit the bull's-eye of a distant target. The strangers nearly always fell for it, and after the money was wagered Jack would smile and shoot the target squarely in the middle. Even realizing they had been had, most of these strangers simply paid up and walked away rather than challenging Jack over the deception.

In spite of his growing reputation as a mean, bad-tempered, quick-triggered cowboy who was to be avoided, some men didn't get the message. Jack was frequently involved in fights. Although documentation is lacking, legends abound that he killed one or several men in barroom brawls while still a teenager. However, if such killings occurred, they were always "justified" by the mysterious Code of the West. No records have been found indicating Slade was prosecuted.

Eventually Jack grew tired of the Texas lifestyle, possibly simply believing he was grown up and that it was time to seek his fortune. Probably late in his teens Jack left his uncle's ranch and drifted westward, eventually spending some time in southern California. There is no record of Jack's West Coast stay, but given his reputation and his history one supposes he continued to fight and drink his way through a number of communities.

Sometime later he is believed to have traveled to what later became Utah and Nevada, probably visiting either Reno or Carson City. Again there is no documentation of such a trip except that in later years, Jack occasionally referred to pleasant memories of the West, especially the Pacific coast and parts of present-day Nevada.

On May 4, 1847 (some say it was May 22), Jack showed up back at Alton, Illinois, a few miles from his childhood home. He apparently went there specifically to enlist in the U.S. Army. The Mexican-American War was just underway, and the young Mexican-hating Slade wanted to be a part of it. Some writers have suggested that Jack's interest in joining the army may have been because he was already on the run from the law. It certainly would account for his sudden patriotism. In actual fact, however, America's bad guys frequently volunteered to wage war on her behalf. (Years later Butch Cassidy and the Sundance Kid were reported to have gone to Colorado specifically to volunteer for the army after World War I erupted, in exchange for clemency. Their offer was rejected. Gangster-controlled unions made sure American ship-building went on at full speed in World War II, and the Mafia is widely reported to have volunteered to help President John Kennedy battle Fidel Castro.)

Accepted by the army, Slade was assigned to Company A, First Illinois Infantry. At the time of his enlistment, U.S. Army records describe Slade as being five feet, six inches in height, with "dark complexion, black eyes and light hair." An officer noted that Slade weighed 150 pounds, was clean shaven, and "very muscular." In spite of the official records saying he had "light" hair, the officer's handwritten notes claim Slade had reddish-brown hair[2] and other descriptions say his hair was jet-black. After some preliminary training, Private Slade and his unit were shipped off to the southwest.

It was apparent almost from the beginning that Jack and the army were not well suited to one another. Some sources say Slade saw action and apparently acquitted himself well while under enemy fire. He also may have spent a portion of his time serving as a military teamster on the Santa Fe Trail.[3] However, Jack remained fiercely independent and resented taking orders from anyone—an attitude that did not amuse several narrow-minded noncoms and officers.

Slade was in the army for a year and a half, and he apparently spent the bulk of that time in the stockade. Frequently these incarcerations were the result of Jack's increasing flirtation with alcohol. At least one writer[4] says flatly that by this point in his life Jack Slade was already a full-blown alcoholic. If he was not yet totally captured by alcohol, at the very least he was often drunk—and when drunk he was always mean and looking for a fight.

Yet Jack was neither always bad nor always in trouble. After a time it became apparent even to the army that when he was left alone with an assignment, Jack would usually carry it out effectively and with enthusiasm. Any job that could be handled by a single individual was completed quickly and efficiently by Private Slade. Only in the company of other men did Jack forget his assignment and feel compelled to demonstrate his fighting ability.

Jack also excelled on those occasions when he was put into a leadership position. Given his reputation and his constant resistance to authority, Jack didn't get many opportunities for leadership. However, on those rare occasions when Slade was put in charge of some project—a situation in which he could issue the orders for others to follow—he proved himself a capable leader. Slade had the ability to size up a situation quickly, assign the right people to handle various parts of the

Jack Slade perhaps was never photographed; cameras were rare on the frontier during his tenure. This drawing, long identified as Slade, is an unusual artistic technique and may be a doctored photograph. Its authenticity is questioned by some. (Courtesy Western History Collection, Denver Public Library)

task, and then encourage and lead and prod until the chore was completed to satisfaction, qualities that would serve him well throughout his life.

On at least two occasions—possibly three—Slade was promoted to the rank of corporal in recognition of his leadership talent and his skill at completing difficult tasks in a timely and acceptable fashion. After each episode he was quickly "busted" back to the rank of private because of incidents involving his volatile temper.

Eventually, Slade's wartime tour of duty was over. He was ordered back to Alton, Illinois, and there was mustered out of

COMING OF AGE   33

the service on October 16, 1848[5]—once again at the rank of private. Like much about Jack Slade, his precise age is hard to pin down. Military records indicate he was eighteen years old when he enlisted, and when he was discharged seventeen months later, records show he was still eighteen.[6] When the final separation papers were signed it was difficult to say whether Jack or the army was the more pleased.

Some say that at this time Jack thought about dropping by his old home in Carlyle and possibly reuniting with his family. If he really entertained such thoughts, he apparently soon thought better of it. He probably wasn't sure the trouble over the dead hobo was finally and definitely a thing of the past and wasn't willing to risk it. He may also have harbored some resentment that his family was so eager to ship him off to Texas instead of standing by him when he got into trouble. Instead of heading home, therefore, Slade once again turned westward.

His exact travels are somewhat uncertain. He may have spent a few weeks or months in Iowa—he later referred to a brief stay in Des Moines—but he eventually continued on his journey toward the western frontier. A February 16, 1849 letter from his stepfather found in the National Archives requests expedition of Slade's application for a land warrant and states Jack was "disposed to go to California...sometime in the month of April."[7] Apparently he spent several months in southern California before deciding that his future lay closer to home. He began wandering back toward the Midwest.

When he arrived in Kansas City shortly before Christmas 1849, Slade was cold, broke, and in obvious trouble. He had no job, food, or warm clothing, and no prospects of getting any. Possibly frightened for the first time in his life, Slade went door to door looking for work. He eventually came to the offices of Russell, Majors and Waddell.

Russell, Majors and Waddell owned the only major freight transportation system spanning the Great Plains from Kansas

City to Denver, Salt Lake, and points west. With several dozen wagons, scores of horses and mules, and dozens of warehouses and relay stations spread across the country, the company had lots of employment opportunities. Unfortunately, this was not the sort of job most men wanted. A "freighter" was required to spend long, lonely weeks on the trail, separated from family and friends. The trips were fraught with dangers, ranging from storms, accidents, and starvation to armed robbery and Indian attacks.

Perhaps it was the danger and the opportunity for individualism that immediately appealed to Jack Slade. He applied for a job as teamster, pointing out that he already had years of experience working with mules and horses while farming in Texas and as a teamster during his army service. Russell, Majors and Waddell was eager to find employees of any kind, and especially those who knew anything about horses and the outdoors. More importantly, Russell, Majors and Waddell needed men who were tough, and Jack clearly was tough. In fact, Jack's rough demeanor and his reputation as a tough guy was most appealing to the company. As one historian points out:

> Wells, Fargo and Company, the Overland Stage Company, various cattlemen's associations of the West and Southwest, and the railroads of the West—notably the Union Pacific and Southern Pacific—who frequently suffered at the hands of daring robbers and rustlers, retaliated by hiring detectives, shotgun messengers and gun fighters to rid the country of such thieves. ... These hired killers were by and large wholly reliable and good. The very acme of this class was Joseph A. Slade.[8]

The young Slade offered some other advantages to the company; he was unmarried and not closely affiliated with any family or group of friends. That meant he would be able to travel freely and was unlikely to resign his position because of homesickness. Not only that, but should something happen to

Jack, the company wouldn't have to explain to—or send money to—surviving relatives. Jack was hired on at a wage of $100 a month, a rather handsome salary at the time.

Not surprisingly, at the time that Jack was hired by Russell, Majors and Waddell, the company was having difficulty finding and keeping drivers and other employees. Few men were eager to face the extreme hardships and dangers of the Great Plains trail. It was six hundred miles from Kansas City to Denver—six hundred miles of open grassland and endless prairie and not much else. Wagon trains braving the desolation of the trail faced hostile Indians by day and equally threatening bandits and rustlers at night.

Indians were the most feared. They apparently loved to capture the wagon drivers alive and then slowly torture them to death over a period of many hours. Teamsters unlucky enough to be caught by the Cheyenne or Sioux warriors were sometimes lashed to the wheel of a wagon and horribly mutilated; sometimes their tongues or private parts were cut off. Sometimes brush and branches were stacked around the victims' legs and set on fire. Remains of victims were sometimes found days or weeks later by another wagon or an army patrol.

But awful as they were, these Indian raids were not a great deal worse than the attacks of the bandits who sneaked into the freighters' camp under the cover of darkness. The thieves stole the horses or supplies and frequently robbed or killed crews of the freight trains during these nocturnal raids. Even worse, the unfortunate robbery victims were frequently left alive—stranded in hostile Indian territory without horses, weapons, food or water. Under these circumstances survivors sometimes simply committed suicide rather than face the almost impossible task of walking somewhere to safety.

Understandably, not many men applied for the work. As a result, Russell, Majors and Waddell was more than happy to find any experienced teamster who was willing to take on the job. Slade must have seemed like the answer to prayer.

It turned out to be a good match from the beginning. The job was a nearly impossible one, but Slade was just tough enough to handle it. More than that, this was a task that required self-sufficiency—the area in which Slade excelled. And because of his experience with animals and guns, Slade immediately became the leader of the two-man team assigned to one of the freight wagons.

From the moment he went to work for the freighters, Joseph Alfred Slade seemed destined to make a name for himself. Slade's first assignment for Russell, Majors and Waddell, shortly after accepting employment in Kansas City, was to drive one of four freight wagons headed from Kansas City to Denver.

The route selected by the wagon master generally followed the Oregon Trail, from Kansas City, across Nebraska, to near the northeast corner of Colorado. At that time the route was poorly defined and highly dangerous. The trail was a series of ill-defined ruts that cut through the prairie grasses in a generally westerly direction and was subject to constant route changes, depending primarily on the current state of mud, ruts, Indian trouble, grazing, and high water along the way.

Near the northeast corner of present-day Colorado, the primary Oregon Trail turned in a northwesterly direction, heading for Fort Laramie (about eighty miles north of the modern-day city of Cheyenne). But the freighters whose destination was Denver left the main Oregon Trail there and turned their wagons southwestward alongside the South Platte River and continued on into the rapidly growing town of Denver.

Getting from Kansas City to Denver was no easy task from the beginning—and rapidly got worse. Sioux, Arapaho, northern and southern Cheyenne, Kiowa, Kiowa-Apache and Ute Indians along the trail increasingly resented the encroachment of the white man. Their mounting frustrations stemmed from years of broken treaties and broken promises. They hated what the immigration had done to their hunting grounds. They also objected to white men claiming ownership of their land and sometimes fencing it off. The whites slaughtered more buffalo than they could use, apparently just for fun. Whites also frequently cheated the Indians in trading deals.

Early on the Indians had tolerated the occasional white trapper or miner who meandered into the region—but as the trickle had become a torrent, the Indians realized that their entire way of life was at stake. There was no end to the problems suddenly thrust upon them by the western migration of Anglo Americans.

Soon the Indians began to fight back. They focused their hostility on the freight wagons in particular. All the fear and hatred felt by the warriors seemed suddenly aimed at the teamsters who drove the freight wagons out across the prairie. Jack Slade was now one of those men.

But Indian trouble was only small part of the litany of terror facing Russell, Majors and Waddell freight trains. When Slade took a job as a teamster for the company, he learned that the last four company wagon trains trying to reach Denver had been attacked by robbers and thieves. The robbers had killed all the teamsters and freighters; they apparently wanted to leave no eye-witnesses who could identify them to the local sheriff.

Slade was well aware of these problems when he signed on as a teamster. Unlike many of the other drifters hired by the company, however, Slade was also fully prepared to deal with such difficulties. On his left hip he wore the sheath carrying his Bowie knife; on the right was a holster holding his trusty new Navy Colt revolver. The other drivers and the four escorts of this first Slade freight train were armed with both pistols and rifles, but Slade did not care for the long guns. He felt the rifles were clumsy to use, difficult to load, and a detriment in time of hand-to-hand combat. The other men in the wagon train warned Slade that he would need a rifle to defend himself on the trail and then made fun of him for thinking he could defend himself with a pistol. Slade ignored their taunts.

Slade was driver on one of four wagons making this trip. This job led to another of the often repeated episodes which added to the Slade legend. Each wagon had a driver and an armed guard; there is no information on who served as Slade's guard. The four wagons were four days on the trail—about a hundred miles east of Kansas City—when Indians attacked. The raid came swiftly and without warning, just after noon.

The freighters had halted at a little stream so the horses could drink and the men could take a breather and eat a bite of lunch. Then, just as the wagons began to move once again, a band of fifteen or so Cheyenne warriors came thundering over a little hill, whooping and hollering and firing rifles at the wagons. Although the braves might have belonged to any tribe or group, it appears likely that they were members of the dreaded Dog Soldiers,[9] the new and deadly Indian warrior society. The startled drivers and guards leaped from the wagons and dived for cover as the Indians raced toward them.

The other three drivers knelt behind their wagons and begin firing rifles at the intruders. Slade and the four guards, however, jumped into a shallow ditch that ran alongside the trail. As the Indians galloped past on their first pass, Jack seemed mesmerized by the attack; he simply crouched and watched as if spellbound. The other white men opened fire—shooting wildly and inaccurately at the Indian attackers.

One of the teamsters was wounded in the hand on this first pass by the warriors. He dropped his rifle and fell back in the ditch, moaning in pain, and unable to help defend the wagons. Others continued to fire, but without apparent effect; the warriors kept coming.

When one of the bullets from an Indian rifle kicked dirt into Slade's face, it seemed to break his trance. Slade shook his head and a look of surprise crossed his face. Then he began to move. And once he began moving, Slade was suddenly a furious whirl of activity.

Leaping to his feet and swearing loudly, Slade stepped out into the trail. Standing spread-legged in classic gunfighter pose, Slade took careful aim at the warriors racing toward him—and blasted one of the Indians from the saddle.

The remaining warriors thundered past Slade and stopped a few hundred feet away. They milled around for several seconds, then began whooping again. Digging their heels into the ribs of their ponies, the warriors raced back toward the wagons for their second attack.

Slade remained rooted in the road. His eyes were mere slits in a face of iron. He stood absolutely unmoving, pistol at his side, watching as the warriors raced toward him. As the raiders came close, Slade finally moved. Taking careful aim at the nearest Indian, Slade leveled his Colt revolter. At a distance of about fifty yards—far "out of range" for a Colt revolver— Slade squeezed the trigger.

The bullet hit with an audible "thud," and the lead Indian tumbled from his pony, crashing in a heap of dust.

Without flinching or pausing, Slade cocked the pistol again. Acting as if he had all the time in the world and as if the target of his bullet were one of those bull's-eyes he so often shot at in west Texas, Slade fired a third time—and a third Indian tumbled from his horse.

The other freighters could hardly believe what was happening. Slade was apparently oblivious to the danger and impervious to the Indian bullets; he simply stood in the road and calmly fired his pistol as the enemy warriors fell dead, one by one.

Slade's calmness and his success seemingly inspired the other men. Now they also rose to their feet and unleashed a volley of gunfire at the Indians. Another of the riders was shot from his horse, and the remainder suddenly pulled up short. Obviously startled by this unexpectedly fierce resistance, the Indians turned and retreated over the hill. This time they did not come back.

After several seconds of silence, Slade walked to where each of the fallen Indians lay. As Slade approached one warrior moved slightly and groaned. Deliberately, Slade cocked his pistol and shot the Indian in the throat. Then as other freighters watched, Slade pulled his Bowie and sliced the ears from each of the dead Indians. Gathering the grisly trophies into a small cloth bag, Slade remarked, "This'll give the chief something to think about."

When the wagon train reached the next town several hours later, Slade climbed from the wagon and began looking around. He eventually saw what he was seeking—an old Indian man who was sitting on a bench near a bar. Slade walked over to the man.

"Do you know the chief of the Cheyenne tribe in these parts?" he asked.

The Indian grunted affirmatively.

"Then take these to him. Along with this note," said Slade, handing the bag and a piece of paper to the Indian. Slade's note read, "I'd love to add your ears to my collection!"[10]

The audacious incident was supposedly witnessed by dozens. True or exaggerated, the story of Slade's incredible accuracy with the pistol, his cool bravery under attack, and his audacity in sending the ears to the chief spread up and down the freight line like a prairie wildfire in October. Jack Slade quickly became a name talked about and remembered throughout the frontier.

Jack Slade had begun to build his reputation as a gunfighter and as a man who would stand for no trouble from anyone. It was a reputation Jack loved and on which he would build his entire life.

Notes on Chapter Two

1. Philip D. Jordan, *Frontier Law & Order* (Lincoln/London: University of Nebraska Press, 1970), 17.

COMING OF AGE *41*

2. Maurice Matloff, *United States Army Historical Series, American Military History* (Washington, D. C.: Office of the Chief of Military History of the United States Army, 1968), 715. Although short in stature, Slade was only a few inches shorter than the average man of his day, so his height was not particularly significant. Observers rarely commented on his height; what drew their attention was his muscular build and his strength.

3. *An Ear in His Pocket*, 7.

4. *Encyclopedia of Western Gunfighters*, 117.

5. *Encyclopedia of Frontier Biography*, 1318.

6. *An Ear in His Pocket*, 9.

7. *An Ear in His Pocket*, 10. If so, Jack was born in 1831.

8. George D. Hendricks, *The Badmen of the West* (New York: Naylor Company, 1970), 105.

9. "Dog Soldiers" began appearing on the Great Plains as warrior societies in the mid-1840s, although they were not unified as a group for another twenty years.

10. *Frontier Law & Order*, 21.

CHAPTER THREE
THE MAKING OF A KILLER

I N HIS FIRST TWO trips across the prairie Slade is reported to have shot and killed a half-dozen Indians and "several" horse thieves. Perhaps more importantly, Slade is said to have trailed, captured and hanged two would-be armed robbers. This was exactly what the freight company wanted—a man tougher than the job. After all, proficiency at out-gunning the highwaymen and Indian raiders was an absolute necessity of survival for the freight companies. They longed to employ the toughest of the tough—men who by virtue of their reputation for a fast trigger finger would make thieves think twice about targeting their company. Slade fit the bill nicely. As one Western historian noted:

> Many small western townships or stage companies would hire the man with the toughest reputation as their sheriff or shotgun messenger or station keeper in order to instill fear into lesser desperadoes, and thereby prevent robberies. Joseph A. Slade was one of the most feared men in the West![1]

Some of Slade's freighting trips with Russell, Majors and Waddell apparently involved hauling military provisions from Missouri to Fort Bridger, Wyoming. In 1857, General Albert Sidney Johnston's command was involved in quelling the "Mormon Rebellion." And the Russell, Majors and Waddell

freighting company held the government contract to supply
Johnston's Expedition. Slade was among the freighters and continued to build on his dangerous reputation.[2]

To reward him for his deadly efficiency—and his growing
reputation as a man just too tough to confront—the company
promoted Slade to his first management position. He was
named stationmaster at Kearney, Nebraska. Within a few
weeks, however, both Slade and the company knew the man
was bigger than the job, and Slade was promoted again—this
time to the position of district supervisor, responsible for all the
company's operations along a three-hundred mile stretch of the
route. Three months later he was promoted again—this time
to the position of superintendent, with responsibilities for five-
hundred miles of trail stretching from Julesburg, Colorado, to
the far southwestern corner of Wyoming—the most desolate
and uncivilized stretch of the entire system!

Unfortunately for Jack and the freight line, not all of Jack's
killings were justified in the sense that his victims were robbers
or rustlers. At about the same time that he was being praised at
company offices for his efficiency in controlling Indians and
eliminating robbers and thieves, Slade chalked up another apparently unprovoked killing—the second documented instance of
him killing another man without reason. Although details of
the incident are sketchy and confused, the killing apparently
took place a few weeks after Slade began his newest job.

Slade was headquartered not far from Fort Laramie, Wyoming. In this current assignment his job description was to
make certain other employees were doing what they were sup-
posed to do and that freight wagons kept moving. He also was
charged with making certain the relay stations were being
properly maintained, animals cared for, and that all the interests of the freight company were being cared for.

Pursuit of that assignment meant personally checking every
relay station on the line. In the course of carrying out that
assignment, Slade accompanied a freight wagon along the trail

and eventually wound up in far southwestern Wyoming, camped near the little outpost of Kemmerer.

Late one evening Slade and one of his employees—a wagon driver—broke out their whiskey bottles and sat around the campfire drinking. As always, alcohol seemed to make Slade tougher and meaner, and to take away his common sense. Soon Jack was looking for a fight. The only person there to fight with was his own employee.

Two cowboys who were riding along the Ham's Fork River later told the local sheriff they heard two men arguing a short distance down the river. The argument quickly grew louder and louder until eventually they heard a gunshot. When the cowboys went to investigate, they found Jack Slade—smoking pistol in hand—standing over the body of the young driver. Like many of the other stories about Jack Slade there is precious little documentation to back up the report—and a lot of confusion as to the details—but it certainly would fit Slade's way of doing business.

One account of this incident claims that during the argument, Slade talked his employee into laying down his weapon so that the two men could fight it out with their fists. When the employee did so, Slade pulled his own pistol and killed the hapless employee.[3]

There is another version of the same killing—one that is more frequently related, although there is little reason to believe one is necessarily more accurate than the other. According to this second version, Andrew Farras (or Farrar)[4] was a sometime-employee of Russell, Majors and Waddell, and had worked for a brief time under Slade's supervision. Given those circumstances Farras probably should have been fully aware of Slade's quick temper and his reputation as a deadly shot. Nonetheless, Farras decided to challenge Slade.

In this version of the incident, Farras and Slade had apparently always gotten along very well, whether driving mule teams across the desolate trails of southern Wyoming or playing cards together in some wayside saloon. It was said that Farras was nearly as tough as Slade himself and was equally adept with a revolver.

As the two men sat drinking and playing cards together at the wagon stop community of Green River, Wyoming, late one Saturday night, their conversation turned to which of them was tougher. Slade said all of his various experiences had made him tougher and meaner than any other man in the West. Farras said that Slade was not as tough as his reputation implied and that other men—including Farras himself—were as tough or tougher.

Their card-game argument quickly escalated, and the men were soon shouting at one another. Finally Farras said to Slade, "If you're so damned tough, why don't you just shoot me? In fact, I dare you to shoot me, right here and now!" Farras leaped to his feet and stood spread legged, staring at Slade through narrowed eyes.

Without hesitation, Slade whipped out his revolver and shot Farras in the heart.

The wounded man tumbled backward onto the barroom floor, a look of surprise on his face. Slade was immediately at his side, cradling his head.

"I'm so sorry, Andy," he said, over and over.[5]

Witnesses said Slade's sorrow appeared genuine.[6]

The shooting had been a foolish showdown between pride and egotism, and as soon as it was over, the victor was sorry. Still cradling Farras's head in his arms, Slade quickly dispatched a messenger "on a fast horse" to ride to Fort Bridger for a doctor. The doctor came within a reasonably short time, but by the time he arrived Farras was already dead.

It's not clear why Slade was never charged with any crime in the shooting death of Andrew Farras. Some writers believe that under frontier justice, Slade was "within his rights" to respond to Farras's foolish dare. Equally as likely, the local sheriff simply had no desire to tangle with a man of Jack

Slade's dreadful reputation. The lawman may have thought it was better to simply let Slade ride away than to challenge him. Whatever the reason and however the death occurred, Slade was not arrested in Farras's death. He quietly rode away the following morning.

If Slade really agonized over the Farras shooting, he apparently got over it quickly. He was said to have boasted about the shooting of his friend on several occasions later that same year while trying to prove that he would do whatever it took to keep his reputation unsullied. In fact, acquaintances said he often bragged about the shooting in later years.

Slade's reputation began to be known throughout the West. In a country already filled with flamboyant gunmen and tough guys, Jack Slade stood out from the crowd. He was more ruthless, more courageous, a better shot, and a worse enemy than any of the others. Slade was soon being described by those who knew him best as:

> ...ruthless and dictatorial, thoroughly honest with his employers and single-minded as to his mission. He arbitrarily ran off crooked ranchers who dealt in stolen cattle or horses, executed stage robbers as he could catch them, treated horse thieves similarly and left bodies hanging as warnings to others....[7]

Another writer says of Slade's reputation; "When sober, Jack Slade was a vicious killer; drunk he was considerably worse!"[8]

Yet, there clearly was another side to Jack Slade—a side that would have amazed most people. This "other" Jack Slade was gentler and more respectable. Many of those who knew him best described Slade as an entirely fair man, a good and loyal friend (so long as you didn't challenge him), and even a good boss. They argued he never shot anyone who didn't have it coming and never fought unfairly.

The West in the middle 1800s was made up of two kinds of men. One kind was like the Jack Slade already portrayed here—tough, mean, gun-carrying, always ready for trouble. These were the men who became famous or infamous in history, who stood out because of the noise they made, and who usually died a violent death at an early age.

The other frontiersmen were considerably more subdued. They were quiet, law-abiding, hard-working. They stayed out of trouble. These pioneers rarely carried guns, stayed out of bars, and tended to live to a ripe old age.

Elias W. Whitcomb, a Wyoming pioneer originally from Westport, Missouri, was that second type of frontiersman. He minded his own business, worked hard, and stayed out of trouble. Whitcomb was a neighbor to Slade when Slade was headquartered at the Horseshoe station, west of Fort Laramie in southeastern Wyoming, at a time when many people believed that Jack was a mean, drunken killer who shot on the least provocation.

On the neighboring ranch, Whitcomb had his share of trouble with rowdy troublemakers, but he said that Jack Slade was never one of them. In fact, Whitcomb wrote that:

> ...So far as my personal experiences with Slade were concerned, I found him a good neighbor, he being one of those characters who if he took a liking to you would do anything in his power for you, but, on the other hand, if he had formed a dislike of you, and should happen to be under the influence of liquor, you were sure to have trouble with him![9]

That's the way it was with Joseph Alfred Slade. He was a classic "Dr. Jekyll and Mr. Hyde". If he liked you, he could be a total gentleman. He was a hard and efficient worker, he tolerated no laziness, and he delivered on his promises. Russell, Majors and Waddell itself said that Slade "...conducted business in a manner satisfactory to the company, and is a man noted for his promptness in all transactions relating to the passenger and express business."

THE MAKING OF A KILLER

But there is no denying that much of the time Jack Slade was also a loud, obnoxious and mean drunk with a quick temper and an apparent total lack of conscience. These characteristics would make Jack Slade one of the most dangerous, interesting and controversial men ever to ride the trails of the old West.

By the mid 1850s, Jack Slade had put in years of hard—and from the standpoint of Russell, Majors and Waddell—entirely satisfactory work for the freight line. During that time he had gained a fearsome reputation all across the frontier. Bandits and Indian raiders thought twice before challenging him or taking any sort of action that might make him angry. In fact, as the forty-year Great Plains Indian war neared its worst period of attacks and killings, the freight line was almost entirely free of such raids. That's a truly remarkable record, given the fact that Cheyenne, Sioux, Arapaho, Ute, Kiowa, and Kiowa-Apache warriors were attacking virtually all other manifestations of Anglo settlement. The freight company attributed its apparent safety to the fearsome reputation of Jack Slade!

By this time Russell, Majors and Waddell Stage and Freight Company had expanded its operation and now had daily stagecoach service between Kansas City and Denver. The company promoted Slade again—this time to the position of "line supervisor," giving him a wide range of vitally important responsibilities. He was in overall charge of the company's Sweetwater Division, the portion of the line that stretched from Kansas City to Salt Lake City. Among his duties was the supervision of twenty or more "swing" and "home" stations, the hiring and firing of all cooks, teamsters, and other help along a two hundred-mile stretch of the trail, the ordering of hay, food, lumber, and supplies needed to maintain company property and equipment, and the coordination of delivery to make certain every station had what it needed on time. All of this was in addition to the responsibility for "…controlling hostile Indians, robbers and other undesirables" throughout his region.

Company records agreed with the general view that when Slade was sober, he was an ideal employee. He was hard working, industrious, friendly, well organized and detail-oriented. Any job assigned to him was done quickly, efficiently and accurately. More than that, he concentrated his enormous energy—and his enormous shooting skill—at improving the company and making it entirely safe from Indians and robbers.

One researcher says that Slade was a logical choice for this tough new job because he was "...fearless, cool, and with excellent executive ability. He as also ruthless, dictatorial, honest with his employees, and dedicated to his job."[10]

But the records also showed that when Slade was "in the bottle"—which occurred with alarming regularity—he was a different man altogether. Those who saw him at such times described Slade as a cold-blooded and heartless killer, meaner than a skunk and more dangerous than a rattlesnake.[11] Even most of his friends soon learned to avoid Jack Slade when he was "in his cups".

Actually, it seemed hardly necessary to point out to anyone that Jack Slade would shoot a man at the slightest provocation. By now virtually the entire West was aware of Jack Slade's unsavory reputation—a reputation Slade probably encouraged because it kept away a lot of trouble. It was a sign of the times that many Westerners considered this tough gun-slinger as a welcome influence on the largely untamed West, and there is no question that many frontiersmen admired Slade. After all, men like Slade helped to control crime and keep hostile Indians at bay; so long as he concentrated on shooting the bad guys, he played a needed and important role in taming the West. And even the mild-mannered, law-abiding citizens of the frontier were quick to cash in on Slade's gun-fighting ability.

After the incident when Farras was killed, Jack Slade was again called on to use his guns and his courage on behalf of his employer. Two successive Russell, Majors and Waddell freight trains had been robbed as they crossed southern Wyoming. In each case, a gang of four masked bandits stopped the wagon train, robbed the wagons and the drivers, stole the horses, took the weapons of the men and then vanished. The wagon train employees were not physically hurt—but they were abandoned in the middle of the vast Wyoming prairie and left to find their way to safety, if they were able.

Now robbery of the freight train was bad enough—but taking the guns and horses of the men was completely unforgivable. Fortunately, the victims in both robberies were able to walk to safety, without having been scalped, shot, or starved to death.

In spite of their safe arrival back in civilization, the freight company was not amused by the robberies. They sent for their enforcer—Jack Slade—and told him to find a way to stop the attacks on company wagons. The simple instruction to Slade was clear-cut; find the robbers and hang 'em.

It was an assignment well suited to the talents of the company tough guy. Slade selected three other men to ride with him, and set out to try to locate the bandits. Both of the robberies had occurred on the stretch of the trail just west of Fort Laramie. Slade rode to the fort and from there began his search.

Within hours Slade struck pay dirt. Questioning bartenders and bar patrons in the vicinity of present-day Wheatland, he learned that four strangers had been hanging around the general area for several weeks. The four careless strangers drank heavily and spent freely and were said to have boasted loudly of having "relieved" travelers of their possessions. Unhappily, no one knew where the strangers were at this time.

For several weeks Slade combed a vast area of southern Wyoming and northern Colorado, searching in vain for the four armed robbers. The search produced no new clues, and some of the men riding with Slade became impatient. The failure didn't stop Slade, however—it merely made him more determined than ever.

Slade figured that if the four drunks he had heard about really were the robbers he was seeking, they would eventually run out of money. When that happened he presumed they once again would come out of hiding in order to attack a passing freight train of wagons.

Having reached that conclusion, Slade went to the nearest stagecoach relay station, just west of Fort Laramie, possibly Nine Mile Station. It turned out to be a fortunate decision. At the station Slade learned that another freight train was due sometime within a few days. He also learned that a stranger had been at the station just a few hours earlier, also inquiring about the due-date of the next freight train.

Slade and his three hand-picked companions rode west from the station and soon took up a position on a high hill not far off the main trail. From their position they could see several miles in both directions along the route of the Oregon Trail. It was a perfect place to watch whatever was going on in either direction—and especially along the isolated stretch of trail that wound through a small canyon below.

Slade cautioned his men to keep out of sight and to restrict their movement. He was personally confident that their manhunt was about to pay off.

In spite of chilly weather Slade would not permit the other possemen to build a fire. Although the lack of a fire meant great discomfort to Slade (and the others), he wanted to be sure that no one would see the smoke and realize someone was hiding amongst the trees up on the hill. Then through the silence of the chilly winter afternoon, Slade simply waited.

The freight train finally put in at the station about mid-morning of the following day—seventeen hours behind schedule. Slade and his men, who had been stiff and miserable, suddenly forgot their miseries and came to life. They watched as the teamsters changed horses and refreshed themselves. Eventually the wagons moved out again—heading down the trail which passed the hill where Slade was hiding.

From his vantage point, Slade watched with mounting anticipation as the train slowly rumbled along the dusty trail.

Within minutes Slade's patience was rewarded. He caught a glimpse of movement in the trees on the opposite side of the trail. Soon he could see four men, moving parallel to the wagons and toward a point at which the trail cut through the narrow canyon almost at Slade's feet. Slade ordered his men to mount up and then quickly headed for that same point.

It took longer than expected for Slade and his men to work their way down from his hillside perch. By the time they arrived at the canyon, the robbers had already held up the wagons and fled. Following their usual pattern, they had robbed the drivers as well as the wagons. The bandits had taken weapons and horses and had then ridden away into the pine-covered hills.

Slade was furious that he had missed the robbers. He told the victims to begin walking back to the station, pointing out that if they moved quickly they could still reach it before supper. The apprehensive freighters wanted Slade and his men to escort them along the trail, but Slade would not hear of it; he had far more important fish to fry.

Now Slade and his companions set out after the bandits. Although the bandits had only a thirty-minute head start, they were difficult to find. Slade pursued them for four hours before finally sighting the men in the distance. All during that long chase, Slade seemed to get angrier and angrier. It was late afternoon before Slade caught up with the robbers.

Confident that they had escaped safely, the thieves had grown careless. Oblivious to the little posse slowly approaching them, the robbers made a camp on a river bank in a small valley about fifteen miles north of the scene of the robbery. Slade's men could easily see the camp from atop a ridge a mile or so away.

Slade signaled his companions to dismount some distance from the robbers' camp. Moving as quietly as possible through the trees and underbrush, the four men sneaked to within a few dozen yards of the robbers' campfire. But this was not the time to attack; it was still daylight, and the bandits had ready access to their firearms. Slade signaled to his men to stay put, and settled down to wait for darkness. The four possemen hid in a grove of trees, fighting off the cold evening air as they patiently waited for the bandits to eat dinner and eventually bed down for the night. Even after the robbers were in their bedrolls Slade wouldn't permit his companions to strike.

As time passed it grew bitterly cold and Slade's little posse was increasingly miserable, but still Slade wouldn't allow them to move. The hours dragged by slowly as the robbers' fire died to a few glowing embers. Finally it was midnight.

At long last Slade silently drew his revolver from the holster and nodded his head, indicating his three companions should move out in either direction. In minutes Slade and his men had silently surrounded the bandits' camp.

Slade leaped over a rock and ran into the midst of the robbers. One of the startled bandits sat upright and reached for a rifle. Slade fired one shot, striking the bandit in the center of the forehead. The robber tumbled backward and fell in a lifeless heap. The other three bandits stood up and raised their hands into the air.

Slade was rarely in a good mood, but he was especially short-tempered this day and in no mood to take prisoners. He ordered the men's hands tied behind their backs. Then without saying anything to his captives, Slade led the robbers to a nearby cottonwood tree. Speaking quietly and without emotion, Slade gave orders to his companions. They took three ropes off their saddles, and Slade fashioned a noose in the end of each. One of Slade's men climbed to an overhanging branch. Slade passed up the ropes, which were draped over the branch and securely tied to the tree trunk. By this time, the three surviving robbers were begging for mercy, babbling out their remorse, and pleading for their lives—but the pleas fell on deaf ears.

One of the robbers said to Slade, "For God's sake, mister, we never kilt no one. There's no call to hang us." And when

Slade ignored the plea, the man added, "If you're gonna kill us anyway, at least just shoot us. Don't hang us, whatever you do." In answer Slade just snorted. He spit into a clump of bushes, then turned toward his own men. Nodding his head, he indicated that the three bandits be put onto their horses. Once mounted, the robbers were led to the tree. Without speaking, Slade placed the nooses over their heads. Businesslike, he carefully checked each rope to make certain it would hold.

Except for the rustling noise of the horses, the night had become completely and eerily silent. The only other noise was the quiet sobbing from the young robbers. Slade appeared not to notice. Eventually, he appeared satisfied with the ropes and other details. Slade walked behind the horses and slapped each animal on the rump. The startled horses leaped forward, and the three bandits were left dangling in the air, kicking and twisting.

Under such circumstances, of course, the necks of the robbers did not break as would have been the case with an execution-type hanging. Instead, the robbers slowly strangled to death while they writhed in agony from the three ropes.

By the time the last man ended his death struggle, Slade had already mounted his own horse and ridden out of camp. He never looked back.

Slade and his three companions rode in silence through the moonlit night, all the way back to the stage relay station. Once there, Slade sent a simple telegram to the Russell, Majors and Waddell headquarters at St. Joseph, Missouri:

"There will be no more robberies.

Jack Slade"[12]

NOTES ON CHAPTER THREE

1. *The Badmen of the West*, 14.
2. *An Ear in His Pocket*, 15.

3. Virginia Cole Trenholm, *Footprints on the Frontier* (Douglas, WY: Douglas Enterprise Company, 1945), 66. It appears that like so many Jack Slade stories, several facts and considerable fiction eventually got entangled into one. Most historical accounts indicate Slade and his employee got into an argument for unknown reasons and Slade eventually shot the employee. There is no solid evidence of him "tricking" the employee or "cheating" in their eventual showdown. This writer identifies the victim here as Andrew Farrar.

4. Many historians use "Farras", but the reliable *History of Larimer County* says the name was "Farrar".

5. *Encyclopedia of Western Gunfighters*, 104.

6. At least one writer claims that this was an even more cold-blooded killing. His version is that Slade was already drinking in the bar when Farras entered, and that Farras challenged Slade to a duel because of some past dispute. He says Slade taunted Farras that anyone could fight with guns, but that it took a real man to fight with fists. When Farras accepted the challenge and laid down his pistol, Slade yanked out his own and shot Farras dead. *Encyclopedia of American Crime*, 664.

7. *Encyclopedia of Frontier Biography,* 1318.

8. Carl Sifakis, *Encyclopedia of American Crime* (New York: on File, 1973), 664.

9. Elias W. Whitcomb "Reminiscences of a Pioneer" (Wyoming State Archives).

10. *Encyclopedia of Frontier Biography*, 315.

11. *Encyclopedia of Western Gunfighters*, 121.

12. Robert Ellman, *Badmen of the West* (London: Hamlyn Publications, 1974). 17.

CHAPTER FOUR

The Surprising Enigma of Jack Slade

J ACK SLADE SEEMED proud of his reputation as one of the most recognized—and feared—gunslingers in the rough-and-tumble West. Virtually no one dared to raise his ire. Whatever Slade wanted, he got. Fortunately for the timid, he mostly wanted to be left alone. Perhaps his preoccupation with being alone gave rise to some ugly rumors about Slade—uglier than even those actually warranted by the truth.

There is no question that when tracking a horse thief or stagecoach bandit, Slade was quick to pull the trigger. There also was no question that he had already killed a number of men. There also is little question that Jack was chillingly cold-blooded on occasion, as when he unemotionally hanged the young robbers on a Wyoming hillside.

There is, however, considerable question about some other parts of Jack Slade's life and reputation. There were ugly rumors in later years—stories that purported Jack Slade had, himself, become an armed robber and cattle rustler. These rumors cropped up well into his career as the hired gun and supervisor for Russell, Majors and Waddell. In fact, these stories were without any hard evidence to support them. Nonetheless, the persistent rumors remained. The allegations dogged Slade throughout the remainder of his life, and although they were based on shaky evidence and hearsay at best, they are a part of the Slade legend.

One of the most persistent rumors claims that Jack Slade turned to robbery to increase his personal holdings. These stories were told for the most part by people who did not know Slade and who had little personal knowledge of any crimes in areas frequented by Slade. They portray Slade as a robber of robbers, sometimes a Robin Hood, stealing from robbers the cattle and other wealth they had earlier stolen from ranchers and travelers in northern Colorado and, more frequently, southern Wyoming.

According to some reports, a New York man who was a passenger on one particular stagecoach produced a gun and robbed the stage which was carrying an army payroll. The bandit reportedly made good his escape with thirty thousand dollars in gold, fleeing into the hills. Historical accounts report several such robberies in the vicinity of the old Horseshoe Stage Station, west of Fort Laramie, Wyoming. This historic station, one of the first in Wyoming, was constructed by Russell, Majors and Waddell after they bought out the old Hockaday-Liggett Stage Line in 1858. Jack Slade was the Division III superintendent headquartered at Horseshoe Station.

Some writers claim that when the bandit fled after robbing a stagecoach near the station, he was pursued by stationmaster Jack Slade. According to these reports, Slade eventually caught up with the bandit and hanged him from the nearest suitable pine tree. At this point, the stories differ. Some hold that Slade hanged the man because he was a crook, and that the money Slade recovered was returned to its rightful owner (the army). Another version is that Slade tortured the captured robber, trying to get him to hand over the money but that the money was never recovered. A third story is that the bandit handed over the stolen money and that Slade himself then hid it, and that the money became a part of Slade's personal fortune.

Those who hold that Slade himself was a robber claim that Slade buried the thirty thousand dollars in gold on Sibley Peak (or Sibley Butte) in the vicinity of the old Horseshoe Station.[1]

Those who give this version seem uncertain whether Slade ever returned to claim the money or whether it remains buried on the hilltop today. Like most of the other, similar stories of lost treasure, this one has triggered many "treasure hunts," none of them successful, or at least not publicly revealed as successful.

A handful of credible historians either suggest that Slade doubled as an armed robber or report suspicions that Slade may have engaged in such activities. A respectable researcher of Wyoming history—C.G. Coutant who wrote the *History of Wyoming*—openly suggests that Slade not only was an armed robber, but the head of an entire gang of thieves:

> It is commonly reported that while in this country [Wyoming] Slade was secretly at the head of a gang who stole horses, robbed emigrants and did murder. ...It is said that the devil is not as black as he is painted, and this may apply to some extent to Slade. He was, however, a bad man, and committed many atrocious acts while in Wyoming....[2]

It is strange, however, that none of these reports are ever attributed to any individual, and none of them has ever been proven.

Other stories have appeared in print from time to time, attributing additional nefarious deeds to Slade. Like the story of the $30,000 robbery, however, they cannot be substantiated. For example, in southern Wyoming not far from old Fort Laramie a rough, wooded area is known as Slade Canyon or Sawmill Canyon. One of the Wyoming histories says that:

> There is a persistent story that Joseph A. (Jack) Slade...was the leader of a gang in this vicinity. Slade and his men are said to have stolen stock from emigrant trains, in many instances selling it back to the owners. *Men who knew Slade well say ...it is quite unlikely he could have carried on such operations. Diligent search has not revealed the caches of gold and jewelry, plunder of the bandits' raids, supposed to be hidden in the canyon.*[3] [Italics added for emphasis]

The truth is that Jack Slade apparently was never officially accused of robbery or thievery during his lifetime; most of these charges appear to have arisen almost exclusively in the twentieth century. In a way it is odd that Slade would be accused of robbery, since he appeared to be naively open and honest about virtually everything in his life, and because the crimes he is known to have committed seem either many times worse than robbery (the multiple killings) or many times less severe than robbery, amounting to vandalism. Slade was reported to have killed more than two dozen men—some sources say more than *three or even four* dozen—and many of them he hanged, tortured or otherwise killed in a horrible fashion. Many of these killings clearly were not justifiable, even under the loose definitions of the Code of the West.

Yet in all the documented history of Jack Slade there has never been any proof that he ever stole anything—not cattle nor horses nor money. Many of those who knew him best insist that in spite of his other faults, Jack was an honest man who, despite his propensity for violence, came by all that he owned honestly. And the truth is that while Jack often gave the appearance of being well off—or at least "comfortable"—he was nearly always broke.

One of the most respected journalists of Jack Slade's day— Oxford University graduate and newspaper editor Thomas Josiah Dimsdale—wrote that Slade:

> ...was a man gifted with the power of making money, when free from the influence of alcoholic stimulants, which seemed to reverse his nature and to change a kind-hearted and intelligent gentleman into a reckless demon. No man in the Territory had a greater faculty of attracting the favorable notice of even strangers, and in spite of the wild lawlessness which characterized his frequent spells of intoxication, he had many, very many friends whom no commission of crime itself could detach from his personal companionship.[4]

Dimsdale noted that Slade died penniless and in debt to nearly everyone he knew.

Slade's primary employer, Russell, Majors and Waddell, never hinted at any suspicion of robbery, cattle, or horse theft or other such crime on the part of their best-known workman. Since the company was quick to accuse several other employees of theft, that speaks highly of Slade's record for honesty. Nonetheless, the robbery charges continue to recur.

Yet for every story about the meanness and cold-heartedness of Jack Slade there were those that defended him. In many cases, even people who knew Slade to be a mean drunk considered him to be no threat whatsoever to honest, law-abiding citizens and even welcomed him as a decent and respectable neighbor.

During the early years of his career, Jack Slade almost always worked alone. He seemed to always do his best work solo—as evidenced by his brief army career—and he resisted the efforts of his employers to team him with anyone else. He reluctantly accepted helpers only when absolutely necessary, and got rid of them as soon as the assignment ended. As a freight line supervisor, he spent the vast majority of his time on the trail, patrolling the Sweetwater branch of the freight line by himself, riding thousands of miles of lonely Wyoming trail and spending weeks at a time by himself. During that time he whipped employees into shape—and just plain whipped anyone else who got in his way.

The men who ran the dozens of isolated little relay stations that stretched across the Great Plains could always tell when Jack was coming—he rode into sight all by himself. Other men often rode in groups for safety from Indians and robbers—but not Jack Slade. He was always alone.

That was about to change!

History is not clear about when or how Slade met his wife, Maria Virginia. She may have been an early settler who was a passenger on one of the wagon trains for which Jack was a driver or trail boss. She could also have been one of the many lonely frontier widows who longed for a strong, brave husband or the daughter of an acquaintance. More likely, she was a dance hall girl in one of the saloons frequented by Slade, or some other soiled dove of the tough young West.

Whatever the truth, Slade fell hard. He was probably first attracted to Virginia's physical beauty, which other men of the day described as outstanding. Most writers of the time were impressed by her stature at a time when a woman's value was measured in how she shared hard work with her man.

Historians disagree about Virginia's maiden name. All agree that later Slade named the Virginia Dale station after his wife, but some maintain Dale was her maiden name while others believe that the word Dale was borrowed from the creek and valley near there. (Later the Slades named their Montana ranch Spring Dale.)

Virginia stood about five feet, five inches tall, and was "well proportioned." Old photographs tend to lend credence to that claim. Virginia had a beautiful face and was sometimes said to have a charming personality.

At a time when women on the frontier had to share hard physical labor with men in order to clear land, tend cattle, and handle the other jobs of ranch life, bulk and muscle in a woman were desirable attributes. Virginia filled the job description well. One early writer's description indicates Virginia had a pretty face and was "pleasingly stout." He described Mrs. Slade this way: "Virginia was rather good looking and about the same age as her husband, She weighed about 160 pounds."

This same writer (and others) indicated that Virginia was sometimes a negative influence on Jack. In fact, he suggests she may have been responsible for some of his many and suddenly mushrooming problems, adding:

> …Mrs. Slade was not altogether a lovely character, often interfering in her husband's business and many of the difficulties he had with people originated with her. …His wife

Virginia Slade was a beautiful woman, apparently loyal to Jack during his life-time, but quick to find new male friends after his death. Her ladylike looks were deceiving; she was quick with a six-shooter and could out-shoot most men. She did not hesitate to use the weapons whenever she felt it necessary. Courtesy Western History Collection, Denver Public Library)

always possessed a great influence over him, even when he was drunk.[5]

One of the stories about Jack being a decent neighbor had to do with Virginia Dale Slade and Jack's drinking problem. Elias Whitcomb said that he was running a general store which was frequented by the Slades:

> Slade often came to my place to play cards and sometimes imbibed too freely; consequently, Mrs. Slade conceived the idea of getting me out of the way, for she thought that if Slade had to go farther for his whiskey she would have fewer quarrels with him. At this time, Slade had gone to Julesburg [Colorado], so the men were left in care of the station and had full sway. Therefore they proceeded to get on a glorious drunk and when in this condition, at Mrs. Slade's suggestion, they proposed to clean me out. McCarty, with eight or ten liquor-crazed men, started to carry out her designs. One of the men, however, got away and immediately warned me of my danger. This man, and also one in my employ, were terribly frightened and they besought me to fly. The former was afraid of his comrades and the latter for his life. We threw our overcoats over our arms and struck for the brush.
>
> My house was burned to the ground, I thus losing all of my earthly possessions excepting a few horses and cattle which were grazing up the creek about 25 miles. ...All that was saved of the stock at the trading store was two half-barrels of whiskey and a box of tobacco, which were taken by the boys to Slade's.
>
> By this time some forty men were assembled about the station drinking, carousing, and, in fact, ready for any wild or bloody work—so when it was suggested to burn the station, one drunken brute seized a fire brand and started for the hay stacks, which were connected with the stables and other out-buildings. ...Mrs. Slade, who was by this time badly scared, wired Slade the condition of affairs, asking

him to make all haste in returning as they had burned me out and were about to fire the station. She was forced to arm herself with a pistol, and going to the barrel of whiskey, upset it, threatening to shoot the first man who approached her. This determined action on her part immediately put a damper on the enthusiasm of the men.

...When Slade heard of the treatment I had received from his men, he was very indignant. He sent for me and talked the matter over. As a result, he discharged every man who was implicated in the affair and offered to help me in any way he could.[6]

Whitcomb's account reveals a great deal about several people. It indicates that Mrs. Slade was not only manipulative, but also capable with a pistol. It indicates that Slade had compassion for his neighbors when they had done him no harm. It also indicates that Slade tolerated no misbehavior from of his employees—a trait evidenced over and over during his life.

But whatever her personality and physique, Slade liked Virginia. Loved her, in fact, and often rambled at great length about that fact. In about 1857 or 1858, Virginia moved in with Jack and claimed to have married him—although both were vague as to where the ceremony was conducted and by whom. No record can be found of their marriage, but the couple began living together and representing themselves as man and wife. There were few who would argue with them over details.

The Slades were always described as a devoted couple. No where can one find a criticism of Jack as husband nor Virginia as wife. She admired his strengths, and he admired her looks. Even more than beauty, though, he probably liked her now-questioned character traits, for in many ways the love of his life was very much like Jack Slade.

Only one account mentions that Slade may have had Indian wives.[7] If he did, the practice was commonly accepted as a tradition of frontiersmen, even the most respected.

It is interesting that the man famous for his individuality thrived on togetherness with his new wife, Virginia. Throughout their married life, Slade was, in fact, thoroughly adoring of his wife and went out of his way to tend to her whims.

One of Virginia's "whims" was to move away from Horseshoe Station. For some reason, Virginia didn't like the station that Jack called home and nagged Jack to move. In fact Virginia may have "wintered" or lived part time in Denver.[8] Jack had the right to live anywhere within his territory and apparently did not argue over the choice of his bride.

Suggesting that Jack catered to Virginia indicates that she was delicate or refined like the Southern Belles of her day and had to live in catered splendor. Nothing could be further from the truth. Virginia—she never went by "Maria"—was a tough frontier woman who could hold her own in about any situation.

As already indicated, she was physically strong. She could—and did—work long days beside her man driving a team of horses. Virginia was often seen working shoulder-to-shoulder with Jack, loading heavy boxes of freight or undertaking any other physical challenge. She helped groom and train the horses, chop the wood, haul the water and any of the many other tough chores associated with frontier life. She apparently managed the station during Slade's frequent absences. In addition, there is some evidence she also helped with the manual labor in constructing or repairing some of the stagecoach stops supervised by her husband.

But probably even more important to Slade was Virginia's other major attribute—she was quite good with a pistol. While her marksmanship never equaled Slade's, it was said she could hit a bull's-eye eight times out of ten from a distance of thirty yards—something most men of the day could not do. There are reports of shooting matches in which Jack finished first and Virginia finished second—and no one else even came close.

Virginia had other meaningful—and important qualities— including some that were more significant to Jack than mere beauty, strength or marksmanship. She was known to have a calming influence on Jack at times and was even called gentle.[9] Specifically, she also possessed great mental acumen. She was an unusually intelligent woman, apparently quite well read. Her ability to think on her feet and carry out complicated plans would serve the couple well on more than one occasion during their marriage. In fact, Jack owed his life to Virginia's cunning, daring and planning. But that incident came later, after they had been married for nearly two years. There were other scrapes with destiny to deal with first.

About the same time that Virginia entered Jack Slade's small circle of friends, Jack made another new acquaintance who would also greatly impact his life. This new "associate" was James Williams, a would-be gold miner and cattleman originally from Greensburg, Pennsylvania. Williams was quite as tough as Slade himself, but with some marked differences: Williams was apparently eager to avoid physical confrontations whenever possible, yet when backed into a corner he was quite capable of defending himself or his friends from dishonesty or mistreatment. In some respects, James Williams was the antithesis of Jack Slade.

Early in 1858, at the age of twenty-six, Williams headed for Colorado to try his luck as a gold miner. Like most of the other gold rushers, Williams was soon cold, hungry and flat broke. He quickly lost interest in mining and began looking for some other way to earn a living. Like most other men on the frontier, Williams was entirely at home around horses and mules, and after searching for some weeks for a new profession Williams eventually signed on with Russell, Majors and Waddell as a teamster.

Williams's first assignment was as a mule skinner in a freight train under the direct supervision of Jack Slade. The men instantly disliked each other and disliked working together, but they had little choice; Slade needed experienced drivers and Williams needed work. It was clear from the beginning, however, that the men were destined to clash.

This particular wagon train of merchandise was being shipped from Julesburg, in northeastern Colorado, to Virginia City, Montana. Slade, Williams, and other men spent two days loading wagons and tying down the loads, checking the horses, and otherwise preparing for the arduous journey. All during that time, Williams and Slade silently bristled at one another as if both knew what was coming. They made it through the loading process without an explosion, but it was apparent that trouble between the trail boss and his newest driver would not be long in coming.

To Jack Slade it was never enough that he had been appointed by his employers as "boss"; he had to physically prove to everyone else that he deserved the title. That "proof" meant that Slade was not satisfied until he had whipped or cowed every man who worked for him, so that there would never be a challenge to his leadership. If a new employee avoided trouble, Slade found ways to create an incident which led to a confrontation. When the confrontation ended it was clear to everyone that Slade was the unquestioned boss.

Generally speaking, these confrontations were not fatal—especially if the employee quickly indicated he had no heart for fighting. If he could make a man back down, that was good enough for Slade because it clearly established his "right" to give the orders. If Slade had to whip an employee in a fight, however, so be it. Jack was good with his fists and seemed to actually enjoy physically beating another man. Whatever it took, the new employee always left the confrontation with a clear understanding that anything Slade said was law.

It was also clear after these confrontations that there would be no retribution and no revenge from any employee who lost such a showdown. On more than one occasion an employee tried to get even with Slade, and in every case that proved to be a fatal error. Each challenger wound up in a crude grave beside some desolate trail. Sometimes it was an unexplained "accident" on a lonely trail. Other times Jack was cunning enough to make certain that fatal showdowns always took place in front of witnesses and that the other man drew his weapon first. Jack was very good at goading an enemy into making a fatal mistake.

All of this, however, was before the arrival of James Williams. Slade's style of "leadership by bullying" did not sit well with new teamster, and he made no bones about it. The young man from Pennsylvania later said that at the time he knew nothing about Slade's awesome reputation as a gunfighter and killer, but Williams did know he would not work for a bully. Although he hated fighting, Williams was tough in his own right and had held his own in all previous showdowns with local bullies. He was not about to be pushed around this time by a man he considered to be a crude, rude, loud-mouthed bully.

The freight train was barely a day out of Julesburg when the showdown came. Historians differ as to the exact subject that triggered the fight. Some say the two hot-tempered men argued over whose job it was to care for the horses when they stopped at a stream. That seems unlikely, since it was a "given" that each teamster tended his own animals.

Others say the men argued over placement of the wagons in the freight train. That may well have been, since the further back in line a wagon was situated, the more dust the driver had to "eat." Additionally, trailing wagons were more susceptible to Indian attack, since raiding parties liked to hit the last wagon in line. Usually the more veteran drivers had earned a spot near the front of the procession, and Williams considered himself veteran by virtue of his ability. If Slade relegated him to the tail-end of the line that assignment may have been the proverbial final straw.

A third possibility reported in some accounts is that the two men argued over assignment of the guards who accompanied the wagons. Some believe Slade positioned the guards so that Williams's wagon was virtually unprotected in the event of an Indian attack. Again, this suggestion is difficult to imagine, since the wagons traveled close together.

Whatever the source of the dispute, it is known that Jack Slade and James Williams argued loudly as the wagons stopped that first evening. Their raised voices soon became raised hands, and then clenched fists. As other teamsters and guards gathered to watch, Slade and Williams squared off near the campfire shortly before dark.

What happened next has been told and retold for 150 years. Even Mark Twain, writes a version in *Roughing It*. But an informed compilation creates a scene like this.

Slade stood spread-legged, looking calm and relaxed, his hands at his side; one hand hung near his holster. Williams appeared to be Slade's reflection—also standing relaxed and ready. Eventually, Slade challenged Williams to draw his weapon. Slade clearly was prepared to shoot down the greenhorn when he responded and fully expected to out-draw this Easterner.

The two men stood ten paces apart and stared at each other for several seconds. There was not a sound, and even the breeze seemed to pause in anticipation. Neither man moved a muscle. Neither blinked.

At last Williams went for his pistol.

Quick as lightning, Slade went for his.

One can imagine the surprise on Slade's face a split second later. Before this champion gunfighter could draw his own weapon, he found himself staring down the barrel of James Williams's Navy revolver. Slade absolutely froze, hand poised over the butt of his own pistol, as Williams defiantly cocked his weapon. Taking a few steps forward, Williams held the barrel steadily at the bridge of Slade's nose. Everyone watching stood transfixed, expecting to see the end of bad Jack Slade. Slade must have expected it, too.

But Slade had not survived this long without being a fast thinker and a smooth talker. He recovered his composure quickly, in spite of barrel stuck between his eyes. Slade's face appeared to relax and a smile played at the corners of his mouth as his hand dropped away from his own holster.

"Jim, I didn't really mean for this to end up as a gunfight," Slade said, acting as if he had never really intended to draw his own revolver. "It would seem a shame for somebody to die over a matter so trivial as this. We ought to settle this thing in a more civilized manner."

The silence continued for several more long seconds with neither man moving a muscle. At last, Williams slowly lowered his revolver and then dropped it back into his holster.

Williams probably thought that ended the matter, but Slade thought otherwise. As Williams holstered his weapon, Slade took a quick step forward and jumped on Williams, driving him to the dirt. Slade no doubt expected to have the younger man fully under control in seconds. Instead, Williams grabbed Slade by the shoulders on the way down and rolled over as soon as they hit the ground.

The two men rolled around in the dirt for several seconds before breaking apart and leaping to their feet. Slade stepped forward and took a swing at Williams's chin. Williams sidestepped the fist and countered with a stiff right that caught Slade on the end of his nose. The blow drove Slade backward, and before he could recover Williams followed up with a left-right combination that knocked Slade to the ground.

Quick as a flash, Slade went for his revolver—but even more quickly, Jim Williams jumped onto Slade's chest. As he did so, Williams whipped a Bowie knife from the sheath at his side. He touched Slade's Adam's apple with the point of the blade as both men gasped for breath.

Once again, the friendly smile crossed Slade's face and he appeared to relax, as if this were all some kind of game.

Lying there flat on his back, Williams straddling his chest with knife poised above his throat, Slade said, "Jim, you're a heck of a lot faster and tougher than I gave you credit for. I'm mighty proud to have someone like you as a friend."

Williams narrowed his eyes for a few seconds and sat motionless, as if trying to decide what he should do. At last he stood up. Slade rose shakily to his feet, blood running down his lip from a broken nose. Williams watched warily and took two steps backward as his antagonist caught his breath, but the fight was gone from the loser of the confrontation.

"Ain't no sense in us fighting," said Slade. "I was just testing your nettle. Why, I could go anywhere, fight any battle, with a man like you at my side. Effective now, you're my second-in-command!" Slade extended his right hand in a gesture of friendship.

Williams looked suspiciously at the extended hand, but did not take it. He clenched his jaw and then spoke in a quiet voice:

> Let's get something straight, Jack Slade. I don't like your way of doin' business. I don't like bullies, and I don't take orders from a man I don't respect. So from now on, I'm in charge of these wagons. I make the decisions, I give the orders. You work for me. If you don't like it, you can start walking right now. And if you stay, I want no trouble from you or I'll kill you quicker'n you can start another fight.

The other men standing around the circle held their collective breath. They expected Slade to go for his weapon again, and for one of the men to die. Amazingly, Slade gave in.

"That's fine," Slade said mildly to Williams, smiling again but looking somewhat shaken. "I got no problem working for you, Jim. Together we can do anything, and it don't matter which of us is givin' the instructions."

"OK, then, it'll be me. I'm the wagon master," said Williams. "An' I also like to have friends who can handle themselves. So from this point on, you're my second-in-command. When I'm not around, you're in charge."

This time, the two men did shake hands.[10]

Incredibly, the battleground agreement actually held, and for the remainder of the drive to Montana things went very well. Williams gave the orders, and Slade quietly obeyed — apparently without grumbling — just as did all the other men on the trip. It was one of few times in Jack Slade's life when he submitted to the authority of another civilian.

When the wagon train finally rumbled into the destination near Virginia City, Montana, a month later, James Williams submitted his resignation to the stationmaster. "One trip was enough for me," he said. "I'm gonna settle here and try my luck at ranchin'."

Slade appeared surprised by Williams's decision—and perhaps a little relieved. For the second time he and Williams shook hands.

"I expect we'll see each other again," said Williams. "I hope it'll be as friends."

"I'm sure it will be," laughed Slade. "We're too good of friends for it to be any other way."

The following morning, Slade turned the freight wagons around and headed them back toward the south. Williams set out in the opposite direction to find his fame and fortune as a Montana rancher.

Notes on Chapter Four

1. *Footprints on the Frontier*, 78.

2. C.G. Coutant, *The History of Wyoming*, volume 1 (New York: Chaplin, Spafford and Mathiesen, 1899), 405.

3. Writers' Program Wyoming, *Wyoming: a Guide to its History, Highways and People* (Chicago: A WPA Project, Bison Book Edition, 1981), 301.

4. Thomas Joseph Dimsdale, *The Vigilantes of Montana* (Norman, OK: University of Oklahoma Press, 1953), 194.

5. *The History of Wyoming*, volume 1, 405.

6. Elias W. Whitcomb, "Reminiscences of a Pioneer" (Wyoming State Archives).

7. Bettelyoun, *With My Own Eyes*.

8. *Ibid.*

9. Robert Ellman, *Badmen of the West* (London: Hamlyn Publications, 1974).

10. This account of the fight is based on several sources, and while obviously every detail cannot be documented it is intended to convey the general nature of the confrontation. Mark Twain gives an entirely different version of this incident (*Roughing It*, 91). According to Twain when Williams got the drop on Slade, Jack said, "It would be a pity to waste life on so small a matter." At that point, claimed Twain, Williams put away his own weapon; Slade laughed, pulled his own weapon and shot Williams dead.

Twain, who wrote with a sort of "gonzo journalistic style," often mixed fact with fantasy if it made his story more exciting. He was clearly in error on this matter, since Williams and Slade were to have a fatal encounter several years later. For the time being, though, Twain's story made better reading for the folks back East. It added to Slade's mystique, and the writers of the day simply could not have a bigger-than-life hero who backed down in the face of difficulty. In truth, however, Twain's version simply was not factual.

Of some interest is the fact that the Twain version of this fight is identical to the description Virginia Cole Trenholm gives of the confrontation between Slade and the man he killed on a western Wyoming riverbank a few years earlier. However, there is not enough evidence to support an assumption that such a make-peace-and-shoot-'em incident ever actually occurred in either of these instances or elsewhere. More likely, this is one of the enduring yarns attributed to Jack Slade without any real supporting evidence.

CHAPTER FIVE

SOLVING THE INDIAN PROBLEM

B Y LATE IN 1858, the Colorado and Wyoming areas were attracting thousands of new settlers. Fur trading was waning throughout the West; but cattle ranching (and cattle rustling) was gaining a foothold. In addition, the Rocky Mountain gold rush was in full swing and new settlements were cropping up in the Rockies. Some of them, in fact, were becoming real cities, with a normal business district and the semi-sophistication that accompanies civilization.

This rush of activity was great news for the transportation and freight business; Russell, Majors and Waddell couldn't build or buy wagons fast enough to handle the demand. The company was expanding as quickly as possible to meet the need. Expansion meant hiring dozens of new employees, buying scores of horses and mules, building miles of new trail and adding dozens of relay stations.

At the headquarters office in Kansas City the company hired its latest stage driver who was assigned in the Sweetwater Division. (Sweetwater Division was basically everything west of Omaha, covering the old Oregon Trail routes across Wyoming and now including the heavily-traveled spur-routes from Julesburg to the booming little mining town of Denver.) The newest driver's name was James Butler Hickok, but he preferred to be called by his nickname, "Wild Bill." Hickok, currently between jobs as lawman and army scout, was assigned as a stagecoach driver, operating in extreme western Kansas, the Nebraska panhandle, and southeastern Wyoming. That meant he worked for Jack .

Before long Hickok met his new boss face-to-face. Unlike so many other meetings between Jack Slade and a new employee, Hickok immediately took a liking to the rough gunslinger that was his supervisor. For some reason the feeling was mutual, and the two men quickly became good friends, even without the normal initiation by fist. Slade apparently admired Hickok's flamboyance and aggressiveness and his great skills with a pistol or rifle. In turn, Hickok admired Slade's ability to get things done. He also admired Slade's tough-guy reputation and admitted to others he was impressed with Slade's uncanny marksmanship with his revolvers.

In spite of Jack Slade's reputation as a loner and a bully, it's not terribly surprising that Slade and Hickok hit it off—the men were so much alike in so many ways. In addition to their skills at fighting and shooting, they also behaved much the same in other ways. Like Slade, Hickok loved to drink—and when he drank, he tended to get very mean.

In an 1883 publication entitled *The History of Greene County, Missouri,* Hickok is described as, "…by nature a ruffian…a drunken, swaggering fellow who delighted, when on a spree, in frightening nervous men and timid women."[1]

Like Jack Slade, Wild Bill Hickok was not above killing another man on the flimsiest of excuses and did so on a number of occasions. One unverified story about Hickok claims he shot and killed three men in Tim Dyer's Dance Hall and Hotel at Sidney, Nebraska, one night in 1857—simply because the strangers made fun of Hickok's hair style.

Within weeks after he went to work for the freight company, Hickok and Slade were friendly companions. The rapid expansion of the line and the proliferation of settlers meant that there was enormous work to be done. Slade and Hickok were literally working side-by-side to control a bevy of problems cropping up all along the line. Rapid growth brought with it a series of new problems and seemed to exacerbate the old ones; there was more theft, more construction problems, more roads to lay out, more goods to transport, and more robbers and Indian raiders to track down.

In the past, such problems happened only occasionally, and when they did, they brought a quick response from Jack Slade. Now, trouble along the line was almost a daily event—but it still got a quick response from both Slade and Wild Bill Hickok. Although Hickok was technically a driver, he soon acted as Slade's second-in-command. He seemed almost as good as Jack at thinking through a problem and devising some scheme to make things better.

Solving the day-to-day problems of a freight line—shortages of animals and buildings and supplies—was not especially noteworthy; scores of men were doing so throughout the country on a daily basis. On the Sweetwater Division, though, there were also problems involving cattle and horse thieves, stagecoach robbers, Indian attacks and a variety of other violent crimes that demanded an immediate—and tough—response. In most of the territory traversed by the Sweetwater Division there was either no local law enforcement authority, or the only lawman within a hundred miles had his hands way too full to follow up on stagecoach robberies in out-of-the-way places. In theory the U.S. Army was responsible for enforcing the law in these wide-open spaces, but it, too, was unable to keep up with the crime and the mushrooming Indian problems.

That left the bigger problems of the freight company to Jack Slade and Wild Bill Hickok. Anytime there was trouble somewhere in the division, Hickok and Slade would show up a short time later. Soon they developed reputations as being men who always found the criminal, usually ending his career at the end of a rope tossed over the limb of the nearest cottonwood tree.

Mark Twain described this focus on tracking, catching, and punishing thieves and highwaymen as a tough one, well-suited to the talents of Jack Slade:

It was a very paradise of outlaws and desperadoes. There was absolutely no semblance of law there. Violence was the rule. Force was the only recognized authority. The commonest misunderstandings were settled on the spot with the revolver and the knife. Murders were done in open day, and with sparkling frequency, and no body thought of inquiring into them. It was considered that the parties who did the killing had their private reasons for it....

Slade took up his residence sweetly and peacefully in the midst of his hive of horse-thieves and assassins, and the very first time one of them aired his insolent swaggering in his presence he shot him dead! He began a raid on the outlaws, and in a singularly short space of time he had completely stopped their depredations on the stage stock, recovered a large number of stolen horses, killed several of the worst desperadoes of the district, and gained such a dread ascendancy over the rest that they respected him, admired him, feared him, obeyed him.

Twain said that one of Slade's most significant characteristics was his absolute refusal to give up until he had solved whatever problems were assigned to him. If those problems involved finding a horse thief, the thief might as well start praying:

...Slade was a man whose heart and hands were steeped in the blood of offenders against his dignity; a man who awfully avenged all injuries, affronts, insults or slights, of whatever kind—on the spot if he could, years afterward if lack of earlier opportunity compelled it.[2]

Over several months, Jack Slade and Wild Bill Hickok solved a sizeable number of difficult "problems" for the stage and freight line. Typically, their solution involved shooting or hanging thieves, suspected thieves, rustlers, robbers, and Indian raiders. As always, there were rumors that on occasion Slade and Hickok also killed people for substantially lesser reasons.

In July of 1861, for example, Hickok (and a couple of other employees) shot and killed three men at the Rock Creek Station in extreme western Nebraska. The three dead men apparently tried to back out of a contract to buy some land from the freight company.[3]

Occasionally, Slade and Hickok ran across and assisted other famous frontiersmen. In his book *The Life of Buffalo Bill*, William Cody tells that when he was a young man he was robbed and taken prisoner by a gang of horse thieves in the foothills on the east side of Laramie Peak. Cody claims to have eventually knocked one of his guards unconscious, shot another, and then fled on foot for his life. When he eventually reached safety it was at the Horseshoe Station of the Russell, Majors and Waddell freight line, where Jack Slade headquartered his division. Cody says Slade was solicitous about his welfare and quickly organized a posse and searched for the robbers, but that the bandits were never located.[4]

Slade was more successful in tracking down the crooks bothering his freight line and in making the line run more efficiently. Hickok and Slade sometimes found it necessary to fire a number of unreliable or trouble-making employees. They also retrained teamsters and other workers to make them more efficient and responsive to changing needs of the company. With his company's blessing, Slade replaced scores of old or ailing horses and repaired or replaced old equipment. Slade and Hickok also supervised construction or repair of several stage stations along the trail, and cleaned up a section of the line that prior to their energetic overhaul had fallen into both disrepair and disrepute. After nearly eighteen months of concentrated labor, the Russell, Majors and Waddell Sweetwater Division was the most efficient in the entire company.

This may have been Jack Slade's finest moment—the only time in his life when he was credited with making a strongly positive contribution to his company and the people he served. It was too good to last.[5]

Many Overland stagecoaches were hastily built to meet a growing demand for transportation. Heavy cloth was all that covered some vehicles, but the rear of the coach was reinforced to allow a guard to ride facing backwards for a better viewpoint. (Courtesy Western History Collection, Denver Public Library)

In the spring of 1860—just when the great Colorado gold rush was reaching its peak and transportation facilities were needed as never before—the freight line was hit by a costly series of deadly Indian raids. (Great Plains Indians, often encouraged by Confederate agents, chose the eve of the Civil War to launch major attacks throughout Kansas, Nebraska, and Colorado.) A dozen drivers and guards were killed and as many as thirty wagons looted and burned in a matter of a few weeks. The attacks were spread out along the Overland Trail from Omaha to Fort Laramie, and appeared to be the work of a roving band of "renegade Indians."

Closer examination indicated that the attackers were Cheyenne Dog Soldiers who were committed to halting the sudden influx of tens of thousand of white immigrants and settlers. While most of the attacks were against wagons traveling along isolated stretches of trail, the warriors also targeted the stations themselves. The isolated stations were seen as an easy source of horses and sometimes of money and other valuables.

In rapid succession starting in March 1860, seven company stations were attacked, robbed and burned to the ground. In each instance, unfortunate employees were captured, brutally tortured, and murdered. The bodies of the victims were sometimes nailed to fences or buildings and left as a warning to others to stay out of the area. Neither company records nor army reports state specifically how many died in these raids, but the number apparently was more than twenty-five.

On at least three other occasions, the Indian raiders destroyed stagecoaches as they pulled out of a relay station. In each of these incidents the men in the stagecoach were killed defending against the attack. They were the fortunate ones.

Women who were in the coaches were kidnapped and brutally treated by the warriors—raped repeatedly, usually by multiple men. Some of the women were later "traded" to other tribes, to undergo still more rounds of brutality. Eventually some of the women committed suicide. A few were later ransomed by army units, but none was ever again the same.

At this time stage and freight lines were using two different types of depots. The "home station" was a large building, sometimes a ranch house, which served simultaneously as a rest area for weary travelers and as permanent living quarters for several staff members. The home stations were often run by a family as a combination livery stable and wayside inn. Weary passengers could spend the night, eat their meals, and clean up after a long, weary day on the road, while employees took care of the animals.[6]

The home stations, thus, were like today's motels. They were vital stopping points for cross country travelers, although they were neither fashionable nor comfortable. Even tough pioneers and settlers who were used to unsanitary conditions must have had some second thoughts about the facilities offered at these home stations. A French traveler described one of these home stations in a letter to friends in Europe:

> At the relay stations you will find waiting a hand-basin and a pitcher of water, with soap and a towel that turns endlessly around a roller. You will find mirrors, combs, brushes, and even tooth brushes, all fastened by a long string, so that everybody may help himself, and no one will carry them off. You might laugh in Paris at these democratic customs; here they are accepted by all and are even welcome, except perhaps the tooth brush, which is regarded with a suspicious eye.[7]

The home stations were located approximately every fifty miles along the Overland Trail. In the stretch between the home stations were located three "swing stations," which were positioned about every twelve or thirteen miles. The swing stations were considerably smaller than home stations. They offered no facilities for the travelers, except a place to get a quick drink of water and a spot to stretch one's legs for a few moments. The swing station's only real reason for existence was as the place at which the drivers could change tired horses for fresh ones. These swing stations were normally attended by only one man.[8] Some swing stations were mere caves or dugouts.

It was these smaller, more isolated and lightly defended swing stations that were targeted by the Indian raiding parties. Cheyenne Dog Soldiers waited until they were certain only one man was around a station. When everything was quiet the raiders routinely swooped down on the station, whooping, and firing their rifles into the building. The lone occupant usually ran to seek cover in some nearby protected spot. Then, while he was kept at bay, the remaining warriors opened the gates and drove all of the horses out of the corral. In minutes, the raid was over.

Although the stationmaster was frequently ignored by these warriors as they concentrated on horses, the Indians sometimes made a point of capturing him, then torturing and killing him. Usually they hunted him down only if he had shot and wounded or killed one of the raiders, or if some member of the raiding party particularly wanted to add a scalp to his collection.

The relay station's buildings were always badly damaged. Occasionally they were burned to the ground—as were haystacks and other company property—and the expensive horses were stolen. It was a nightmare for the freight line.

As the raids continued throughout western Nebraska, the extreme southeastern corner of Wyoming and the northeastern corner of Colorado, the United States Army ordered General Samuel Curtis to stop the attacks. The timing in this case was most inopportune. Curtis had also just been given command of the "Division of the Missouri" and was responsible for preparing the defenses of the entire western two-thirds of the United States in the event of Civil War. Most people already assumed that war was inevitable, and war preparations demanded all of Curtis's attention.

The upshot, of course, was that Curtis had neither the time nor the manpower to chase raiders—even when they were chalking up a growing list of victims. On several occasions General Curtis sent word to Russell, Majors and Waddell that "as soon as practical" he would send troops into the field to track the raiders, but that time was always somewhere in the future. Circumstantial evidence indicates that the Dog Soldiers were being armed and trained by Confederate agents in an effort to preoccupy the United States Army on the eve of the Civil War.[9]

Russell, Majors and Waddell decided they could not wait on the army to help them control the raiders. They turned to the one man they knew who single-handedly might be able to stop the raids. That man, of course, was Jack Slade. The company told Slade that they were unconcerned about Indian attacks occurring elsewhere on the frontier, but that the Indians were to be "thoroughly discouraged" from attacking Russell, Majors and Waddell property, whatever it took to deliver that message.

Slade studied the Indian problem briefly and then concluded he needed only four men to find and "discourage" the responsible Cheyennes, and stop the attacks on company property and employees. Not surprisingly, the first man he chose to assist him was Wild Bill Hickok. He then chose three others from various places in the company—all of them known for their skills on the trail and with firearms—and sent instructions that all were to meet him at Julesburg, Colorado. Julesburg, the home of Fort Segwick, was also the site of the company's newest, largest, and most important home station in the Sweetwater Division.

The Julesburg station was managed by Jules Beni[10] (some historians say "Reni", or occasionally, "Bene")—a hard drinking, tough, and thoroughly unlikable task-master. Although technically in charge only of this home station, Beni had used his fists and guns to virtually seize control of a huge section of the route. One western researcher said of Stationmaster Beni:

> He founded the town, gave it his name. As agent for the Overland, he ruled the division as he had his town—as if it belonged to him. He had overcharged passengers for meals and lodging and had pocketed the money; he had used company hay and stock on his ranch and dared any man to mention it; he was a thief, a liar and a braggart.[11]

Around the Julesburg home station had grown a sizeable cluster of homes, several bars, a livery stable, two hotels and a general store. The settlement sported a permanent population of upwards of two thousand persons—sizeable for its location—and had become known as Julesburg in "honor" of the hated stationmaster. With Jules Beni as the leading citizen it was not surprising that the village was reputed to be one of the toughest places in the entire West. The town's bar was a gathering place for rustlers, robbers, idlers, drifters, and gamblers, and a killing a day in the community was not uncommon.[12]

Originally Jack Slade traveled to the Julesburg home station apparently for the sole purpose of hunting Indians raiders.

If he personally knew Beni prior to his arrival, there is no indication of it in company records or other historical documents. Since Slade had been concentrating for several months on other portions of the Sweetwater line, it is quite likely he had never met the stationmaster, who had been hired by the company only a few months earlier. Upon his arrival in the community Slade apparently met Beni for the first time. It was not a good meeting.

Slade instantly developed an intense dislike of Beni. This was not the normal run-of-the-mill Jack Slade dislike of strangers—this was an all out hate. Slade thought Beni was a dangerous liar, a man who could not be trusted. And the feeling, apparently, was entirely mutual. Employees and townsfolk say that during the brief time Slade was in town that spring, "hostility was so thick you could cut it with a knife." Slade and Beni exchanged sharp words on several occasions and had Slade remained in town much longer there is little question the men would have squared off.

Fortunately, Slade had more pressing things to do at that particular moment than to solve a dispute with the bullying local stationmaster. In a few days, all four of Slade's hand-picked companions had arrived in Julesburg and equipped themselves to go after the Indian raiders.

At just about the time they got organized, one of the company's relay stations between Julesburg and Cheyenne, Wyoming, was attacked by the Cheyenne Dog Soldiers. The stationmaster escaped and even the buildings were not badly damaged, but six fine horses were stolen.

Slade's group headed out on the trail at once—moving northwestward toward Cheyenne. It is said that as the party rode out of town Slade turned to Wild Bill Hickok, and commenting on Jules Beni, said, "I'm gonna have trouble with that man!"

Slade was methodical in his search for the Cheyenne warriors. Questioning settlers, teamsters, and others along the road,

Slade soon picked up the trail of a small band of the Indians who most likely were the raiders. Piecing together bits of information from travelers and settlers and clues left by the raiding parties, Slade's posse determined that there were seven to ten warriors in this particular group. The warriors were heavily armed, and all were riding "fine ponies." In addition to the most recent attack northwest of Julesburg, these Indians were also suspected of being responsible for a recent raid on another small relay station a few miles further up the trail. The earlier raid had not been successful because a half dozen local cowboys happened to be in the area at the moment of the raid and raced to the station. The attackers saw the cowboys coming and broke off their attack, fleeing into the nearby hills.

As Slade worked his way toward Cheyenne, he continued questioning local residents and travelers, piecing together bits and pieces of information. He eventually learned from employees and ranchers that the Indians were now believed camped somewhere north of Cheyenne.

For more than two weeks, Slade's little posse scoured the countryside, picking up additional information but failing to make contact with the warriors. At last, though, by pure chance they stumbled across an Indian campsite which apparently had been vacated by the renegades only a few hours earlier. Hoofprints in the dust indicated the Indians were moving toward the west. The hoofprints also showed that these Indian ponies were shod—indicating the animals were stolen. Slade was certain he was finally getting close to his prey. He and his posse took off in pursuit.

Since no one had pursued the raiders up until this time, they most likely felt completely safe, perhaps even arrogant. At the precise moment Slade discovered their just-abandoned campsite, the Indians were launching another raid and were now only thirty minutes ahead of the posse. This time the Cheyenne warriors hit a Russell, Majors and Waddell swing station located fifteen miles west of Cheyenne.

Unlike some earlier, bloodless raids on these small stations, this time the stationmaster was wounded in the shoulder and the building was badly shot up in the attack. The nine Indian attackers stole eighteen horses and fled southeastward—back along the same trail they had followed to the station. The raiders had gone only a short distance when at the crest of a hill they came face-to-face with Jack Slade and his posse.

Gunfire erupted at once. The men in the posse, men who had been hand-picked by Slade because of their shooting accuracy, were better armed than the Indians. They also had been prepared for a gun battle and had been anticipating the encounter, while the Indians were taken completely by surprise.

The gun battle lasted only a few minutes. When the shooting stopped and the smoke cleared, three Indians lay dead. Two others had been wounded, and four more disarmed and captured.

One of the injured survivors—a minor chief—was soon identified as the leader of the raiders. When it became apparent that he was responsible for the attacks, Slade simply stuck his pistol into the man's face and squeezed the trigger. The shot hit the Indian between the eyes and blew off the back of his head.

Showing no emotion whatsoever, Slade turned to face the remaining captives. He ordered the five surviving Indians (including those who were wounded) hanged on the spot. The Indians were quickly bound and put onto their horses, then led to the nearest suitable tree. True to their tradition, the five condemned warriors sat stoically, watching as the preparations were made to hang them. The posse worked quickly and efficiently, as if going about the routine work of loading a wagon or repairing a corral. They fashioned nooses, looped the ropes across appropriate branches, and swatted the horses. The five Indians struggled for several minutes before the last one died and finally hung limply in the afternoon breeze.

One of the possemen suggested that the bodies probably should be cut down.

"Naw, leave 'em there as a warning to any other Redskin in the area who might have ideas about stealing horses from the freight company," Slade said. "They'll get the message."[13]

Incredibly, the Indians did get the message. Although Cheyenne Dog Soldier attacks would plague the area for another sixteen years or more—with hundreds of attacks on white settlements, ranches, and other freight lines—they almost never again attacked a station or coach of Russell, Majors and Waddell. Such was the reputation of Jack Slade.

Notes on Chapter Five

1. *Historical Atlas of the Outlaw West*, 91.

2. Mark Twain, *Roughing It*, 88–90.

3. *Historical Atlas of the Outlaw West*, 104.

4. *The Life of Buffalo Bill*, 109–118.

5. *Encyclopedia of Frontier Biography*, 1318.

6. Ubbelohde, Benson & Smith, *A Colorado History* (Boulder: Pruitt Publishing Company, 1982), 80.

7. Ft. Collins(Colorado) Museum notes, written by Richard S. Baker, Colorado Historical Society, c. 1988.

8. *The Hanging of Bad Jack Slade*, 24.

9. For a complete discussion of the Confederate Indian strategy, see Bob Scott, *Blood at Sand Creek* (Caldwell, ID: Caxton Printers, 1994).

10. There is considerable difference of opinion as to the correct name of Jules Beni. A few historians, including Jay Monagham, author of the respected *Book of the American West* (NY: Bonanza Books, 1978), 291, call him "Reni" and many others call him "Bene." Original company payroll records of Russell, Majors and Waddell and an original land deed regarding property owned by him near Julesburg use the "Beni" spelling; see Gerald R. Williams, "The Man that Made Jack Slade Famous," *Colorado Historical Society* magazine XXIV (May, 1933): 77. In addition, the *Encyclopedia of Frontier Biography*, 286, says that while many refer to him as Bene, "the correct name is Jules Beni." His name is reported as Bene in numerous other Western publications, including *Badmen of the West*; *Encyclopedia of Western Lawmen and Outlaws*, 285; Joseph Rosa's *The Gunfighter*, 22, and others.

The name issue was also discussed in a Julesburg newspaper article published about twenty years after his tenure in the city. The article, apparently written by a local newspaper reporter, was included in an August 1934, letter from a local writer named Don R. McMahill to a Nebraska historian named J. G. Masters. The article notes that "Beni's name is often inaccurately reported in a variety of spellings, including 'Reni' and 'Bene'. Land records at the Sedgwick County Clerk's Office and original clippings from the local newspaper indicate 'Beni' is the correct spelling."

11. *Encyclopedia of Western Gunfighters*, 286.

12. *A History of Larimer County*, 417.

13. *Ibid.*, 417.

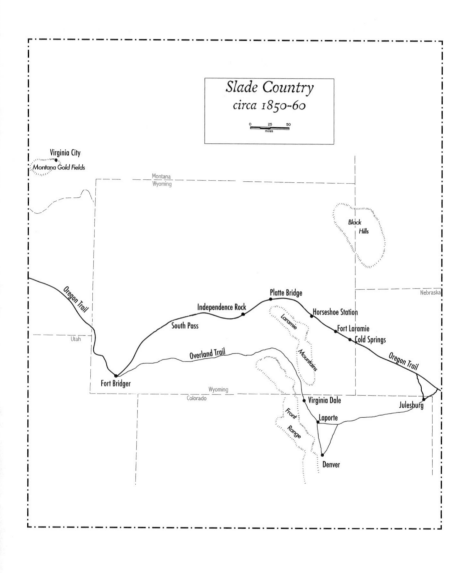

Slade Country
circa 1850-60

0   25   50
miles

Virginia City
Montana Gold Fields

Montana
Wyoming

Black
Hills

Oregon Trail

Nebraska

Platte Bridge

Independence Rock   Horseshoe Station

South Pass   Laramie   Fort Laramie

Cold Springs

Utah

Overland Trail   Mountains   Oregon Trail

Fort Bridger

Wyoming   Virginia Dale   Julesburg

Colorado

Front
Range   Laporte

Denver

CHAPTER SIX

AN EAR FOR TROUBLE

THE "WILD WEST" was changing quickly. Men struck gold and went from rags to riches overnight—or their luck ran out, and they went from moderate sustenance to starvation overnight. The fates and fortunes of the gold fields were completely unpredictable, and the only constant on the frontier was rapid change.

Thousands and then tens of thousands of persons flocked to Colorado's towering mountains between 1859 and 1861, determined to take their shot at fame and fortune. Denver's permanent and temporary population skyrocketed from a few hundred to nearly 100,000 persons in a period of just a few months, and other sizeable communities sprang up overnight in other parts of the West.

This explosive influx of people and the growing conflict of the Civil War greatly impacted both men and businesses on the frontier. So did the uncertainties of mushrooming warfare with Indians, robbers and horse thieves.

One of the more visible changes was that the mushrooming town of Denver suddenly became a major stopping point on the Oregon and Santa Fe Trails—although neither passed within two hundred miles of this gold-rush city. Freight and stagecoach companies scrambled to find the men and equipment to handle Denver's shipping and transportation needs, and the influx of miners plus the businesses to support them dramatically changed the face of the Mountain West.

No longer were the Oregon/California Trails that crossed Wyoming from Nebraska to Utah and Idaho the most important transportation routes of the era. It was now most important to find a way to get goods and people from Julesburg to Denver via a new off-shoot of the Overland Trail route and to create a roadway from the Santa Fe Trail to Denver by branching off near Bent's Fort.

The boom for Slade's employers began even before late 1858 when gold was first discovered on Denver's Little Dry Creek. By the time word of the discovery leaked out, Russell, Majors and Waddell were already well entrenched as the first and largest operators of stagecoach and freight lines in the West. A few months before the first gold strike the company had been awarded the lucrative federal contract to haul military provisions and supplies from Kansas City to points as far west as the Utah Territory (encompassing both modern day Utah and Nevada). Not surprising, then, that Russell, Majors and Waddell quickly also became the single most important freight line for the hauling of mining supplies and other provisions to Denver and the surrounding area.

That sudden shift in focus for the company not only altered business plans, it also dramatically altered the life and priorities of men like Jack Slade. Because the Colorado Rockies were virtually impenetrable, the highways to the west coast had ignored the Colorado area before this time. Now, Colorado suddenly became of utmost importance. Slade was responsible for the building of miles of new trail, three dozen new relay stations, hiring of additional men, buying more horses and generally tending to this suddenly critical portion of the company's operation.

With the new emphasis on travel from Kansas City (at the edge of "civilization") to Denver (at the edge of the gold fields), William Russell of the Russell, Majors and Waddell, through a series of complicated financial and personal maneuvers, joined with others to create a related company known as the Leavenworth and Pike's Peak Express Company. While the company would continue to haul freight, its main interest was in the rapid transportation of people. Jack Slade and most of the other employees in Wyoming were assigned to duty with this new company. The main purpose of the new stagecoach company was to provide daily service from Kansas City direct to Cherry Creek, Auraria, and Denver. The coaches would bring to the frontier thousands of miners, businessmen, ranchers, saloon girls, gamblers, drifters, and others seeking a new life in the blossoming West.

This new stagecoach company owned forty coaches, each capable of carrying up to eight passengers. Each rider paid between $100 and $125 to make the one-way trip from Kansas City to Denver. The price of the ticket included meals. Initially, the bone-jarring trip from Kansas City to Denver took twelve days, although within a year roads and stations had been improved to the point where a traveler could cover the distance in a mere week.

After a few months, however, the booming new freight and passenger line was sold by the parent company to the new Central Overland California and Pike's Peak Express Company, a competitor from San Francisco. The name of the new company was so long and unwieldy that it was usually referred to as the "COC and PP," an unfortunate acronym, or the Overland. The company was badly over-extended and soon encountered serious financial troubles. Freight drivers began saying that the initials "COC and PP" stood for "Clean Out of Cash and Poor Pay." Struggling to survive and cash in on the suddenly flourishing market, the cash-poor COC and PP founded and operated the short-lived Pony Express, and thus gained lasting fame before going virtually bankrupt and finally collapsing in 1861.

When things soured, the COC and PP sold the company's assets to Ben Holladay's new Overland Mail and Express

Company. The newest owners of the line, in turn, pioneered and built much of the famous Overland Trail which soon crisscrossed most of the West. The new trail linked the eastern part of the old Oregon Trail to the important new towns cropping up throughout the frontier. A leg of the new Overland Trail followed the South Platte River from Julesburg to what was suddenly the biggest city in the region—Denver—then it turned northward and skirted along the eastern face of the Rockies to near present-day Laramie, Wyoming. (Laramie, or Laramie City as it was first called, is not to be confused with Fort Laramie. Fort Laramie is eighty miles north-northeast of Cheyenne; Laramie is about fifty miles west of Cheyenne.) Near today's Laramie, the new South Platte leg rejoined the Overland Trail. This new north-south route linking Denver to existing east-west trails became of prime importance to Jack Slade for the next several years.

Shortly after the latest owners of the line had firmly established new routes, they began to have bigger problems than ever before with robberies and thefts. It seemed that almost every major freight train traveling through northern Colorado or southern Wyoming was being attacked by robbers. Swing stations were having horses and supplies stolen with regularity.

Worse than the thefts, several wealthy travelers on stagecoaches were hit by armed robbers. On several occasions the bandits called the travelers by name. It appeared as if the thieves and bandits had inside information. They seemed to know well in advance each time a fat, wealthy freight train or a stagecoach filled with well-to-do travelers would be passing along a given stretch of the route.

In the face of these continuing and most embarrassing robberies, the general superintendent of the freight line, Benjamin F. Ficklin, began to suspect some of his own employees might be involved. His suspicions grew substantially when three successive freight trains carrying secret shipments of gold, money, or other easily converted merchandise were attacked on lonely stretches of trail in the general vicinity of Julesburg, Colorado.

But these troubling robberies weren't Ficklin's only problem. Horse thieves also started showing up at the various relay stations, precisely at the moment that each of the stations happened to have the most and best animals in the corral.

As Ficklin studied the problem, he eventually reached a most troubling conclusion. In a secret report to the board of directors, Ficklin stated his belief that Stationmaster Jules Beni and his staff at Julesburg simply had to be involved in this outburst of skullduggery. There was, he concluded, no other explanation for the series of "coincidences" that always left the thieves with the bulk of the company's most expensive property.

As stationmaster, Beni was routinely notified in advance of VIP travelers, major shipments, and other items that were attracting the attention of the bandits. He also knew when fresh new horses or mules were stationed along the route.

Ficklin began to dig deeper into Beni's background. A check of company files showed that Russell, Majors and Waddell had received numerous letters from Julesburg citizens complaining about Jules Beni. Almost all of the letters complained about Beni's bullying, his trigger-happy ways, and his general rude treatment of local citizens and travelers. Many of the letter writers went a great deal further, however, suggesting that Beni was something far worse than a law-abiding and trustworthy employee. In fact, some local residents were outspoken in suggesting that Beni was a crook. Several letter writers said that Beni was "... a sour individual, not above using company property for his own purposes".[1]

Faced with this mounting evidence against Beni, in late 1859 Ficklin summoned his top trouble-shooter—Jack Slade —to a meeting at Fort Leavenworth, Kansas. At the conference Ficklin laid out all the evidence. He told Slade that he was suspicions that Beni was behind the robberies and horse rustling. After carefully documenting his concerns Ficklin asked Slade to "solve" the problem. "Solving the problem" meant going to Julesburg to personally investigate the staff there, and then doing whatever Jack Slade thought appropriate to end the problem.

Ficklin warned Slade that the job could be a nasty one. It was always dangerous to track criminals, and it could be more difficult when the criminal was a reasonably high-ranking company employee. In his position, Beni would most likely already know of the company's suspicions, and he might set up an ambush for whomever came to investigate. Ficklin warned Slade that things could get violent.

If Slade was concerned about the possibilities of trouble, he gave no indication. Brushing aside the warnings he readily accepted the assignment. Since Slade already disliked and distrusted Beni because of their one brief prior meeting, he may even have looked forward to this assignment. Although Slade's motives and thoughts are unknown, he certainly must have felt triumphant as he headed toward Julesburg for this criminal investigation.

Accompanying Slade to Julesburg was Green M. Thompson, another veteran Russell, Majors and Waddell employee. Ficklin planned to install Thompson as the new Julesburg stationmaster, once Slade got enough information to justify the dismissal or jailing of Jules Beni. Before leaving Leavenworth, Slade also hired an ex-teamster and sometimes drifter named Luke Carson to assist in the investigation of the Julesburg thefts. The fact that Carson had recently been fired by Jules Beni no doubt added fuel to the already smoldering relationship between Beni and Slade.

Like most of the other big events in Jack Slade's life, there ˹e several versions of what happened next. The most likely ˹ion is as follows:

˹ade and his companions rode unannounced into Julesburg, ˹oms at the local hotel, and then began hanging around ˹ bar, chatting with area residents. Slade didn't tell any- ˹ulesburg why he was in town—at least not officially.

On the other hand it appears likely that the reason for his appearance was not much of a secret.

Slade had been in Julesburg only three days when Jules Beni received word that Slade was telling people around town that Beni might be a crook. Beni was infuriated at the rumor and at the personal insult that went with it. He didn't like Slade to begin with, and now Slade was accusing him of crime. Under the Code of the West, that gave Beni the right to silence Slade any way possible—including gunfire. Beni grabbed a double-barreled shotgun from the rack behind his desk and went out looking for Jack Slade.

Unaware that he was now being hunted, Slade was walking out of a local tavern late one afternoon when he almost literally ran into the fuming Jules Beni. Without a word, Beni raised the shotgun and fired both barrels. The blast caught Slade in the chest and abdomen, knocking him backward several feet. He flew off the wooden sidewalk and crashed heavily into the dirt street, face first. As citizens scurried for cover Beni calmly reloaded the shotgun, mumbling all the time in a voice too quiet to be understood by others in the area. Finally the weapon was rearmed. Beni took careful aim and fired two more blasts into Slade's back from a distance of no more than eight or ten feet. Then as an unbelieving crowd watched in horror from behind wagons and around doorways, Beni calmly reloaded the shotgun again and fired a fifth time.

Satisfied at last, Beni lowered the smoking shotgun and stood staring at the bloody and unmoving body of Jack Slade. Slowly, local citizens crept from their hiding places and approached the gunman and victim in the middle of the street.

Without taking his eyes off the bloody heap in the road Beni spit into the dirt and then spoke. "Bury 'im," he snapped to the crowd. Some versions of the story quote Beni as saying, "There's a freight box at the station you can use to bury him." [2]

Beni (and everyone else!) was startled when the "dead" Jack Slade raised his head a few inches off the dirt and muttered

An artist's drawing of Julesburg, Colorado, when Jack Slade was bushwhacked. The stage station is the wooden structure at left-center of the photograph. (Courtesy Western History Collection, Denver Public Library)

softly, "I shall live long enough to wear one of your ears on my watch guard. You needn't trouble yourself about my burial!"[3]

If this version of the story is true—and it is the version most widely reported—there is some question why Beni didn't reload and fire again, finishing the job. Perhaps by now there were too many citizens gathered around to permit such action. Even the liberal Code of the West didn't permit continuing to shoot a man once he was down and apparently dying.

A less-likely second version of this story is also a part of folklore, frequently repeated, and also completely undocumented. This account holds that after arriving in Julesburg Slade and one of his companions began tracking stolen horses. Their search soon led to the ranch northeast of Julesburg, owned by Jules Beni. In this version of the story, an unarmed Jack Slade (or at least Jack Slade with his pistol holstered) and his companion rode to the ranch and found several horses in Beni's corral bearing the Overland brand. Slade then walked to the ranch house to confront Beni.

Beni apparently had been watching Slade since his arrival at the ranch, however, and was waiting for him. Just as Slade raised his hand to knock, Beni jerked open the door and began firing. His first shot hit Slade in the shoulder and spun him around, the second caught Slade squarely in the back. As he fell face-first to the ground, Beni fired three more shots into the body. Then Beni raced back inside his house, re-emerged with a double-barreled shotgun, and fired both barrels into Slade's prostrate body.

Slade's companion raced to his stricken boss, hoisted him onto a horse, and sped into town with him. In this version of the bushwhacking, Jack was taken to the home station and there was awaiting medical attention when Beni showed up and ordered the crowd to "bury him" in the packing crate.[4]

Neither reports of the U.S. marshal nor local newspaper stories give any indication which (if either) version of this story is correct, although subsequent events and company records give far more credibility to the first version. What can be reported with certainty is that Slade was shot several times at close range with a double-barreled shotgun fired by Jules Beni. It is also certain that in spite of the injuries which were severe enough to have killed an ordinary man, Jack Slade survived the attack.

When Slade raised his head and told Beni that he needn't worry about burial—wherever that incident occurred—all writers agree that Jules Beni looked surprised. Some say he made a move as if to fire yet another shot—but then changed his mind. Whether that part of the story is true is a moot point. Spinning around, Beni started to walk away. But even as violent and untamed as was the town of Julesburg, local citizens could not tolerate such cruel treatment as repeatedly shooting a man who had never even drawn his weapon. Several men in the crowd produced revolvers and pointed them at Beni. In a seconds the crowd had taken Beni prisoner.

Beni seemed genuinely surprised at the crowd's angry reaction to the shooting of Slade. He dropped his weapons and raised his hands, at the same time pleading with them to let him go. Beni argued that Slade was known throughout the West as a bully, a trigger-happy gunslinger and a ruthless killer. He said Slade deserved to die.

The crowd thought otherwise. Instead of letting Beni go, someone produced a rope and fashioned a noose in the end, then slipped it over Beni's head. The other end of the rope was tossed over the cross-bar of a telegraph pole. Without a word to the victim, the crowd shoved Beni into position directly under the telegraph pole. Someone nodded, and a dozen men pulled on the rope. Jules Beni was hoisted into the air. He gasped for air and eye-witnesses said his face turned blue.

Fortunately for Beni, company president Ben Ficklin had arrived in town just moments before the shooting after apparently having decided to personally follow-up on the Beni investigation. As Ficklin stepped down from the stage at the relay station, someone told him what was going on at the edge of town. Ficklin raced to where the crowd was in the process of lynching Beni. Ficklin pulled his revolver and fired two shots into the air. The noise startled the crowd into silence. Ficklin ordered them to stop the lynching, and when no one moved he fired a third shot into the air. That finally brought the crowd to life.

Beni was lowered to the ground and the noose around his neck was loosened. The stationmaster who had literally been only seconds from death, lay gasping for breath, his face black and contorted.[5]

Ficklin walked over to Beni. He stood over his stricken stationmaster and said (loud enough for everyone in the crowd to hear):

> Beni, you're a rattlesnake and you've got no right to live, but I don't intend to be party to no lynchin'. If you were to promise to leave the Colorado Territory and never come back or to bother the company in any way, I'd cut you loose right now. If I don't get your promise, though, I'm gonna just stroll away from here and let the crowd do whatever they want.

Beni was grateful for the reprieve, groveling at the feet of his rescuer.

"I promise, Ben," he gasped. "Just let me go, and you'll never see or hear from me again."

Ficklin dropped his six-gun back into the holster and ordered the crowd to release Beni. They reluctantly complied.

Beni staggered to his feet and walked hurriedly but unsteadily to his own horse, which was tied at the relay station. Without another word he mounted the horse and quickly rode out of town to the northwest, heading toward Wyoming.

With Beni taken care of Ficklin finally turned his attention back to Jack Slade. Slade was still lying in the middle of the street in front of the saloon. Ficklin still thought his next job was to bury Slade, but as he approached the "dead" man Slade incredibly again began to stir once again. No one in the crowd could believe that this dusty, bloody mound in the street was not dead—and yet Slade was clearly gasping for breath and fighting to stay alive.

Several men picked him up and carried Slade to the relay station. In the main office Slade was placed on a wooden table. The town doctor was summoned, but he was not optimistic about Slade's chances of survival. The doctor told Ficklin that Slade could not possibly live more than a few minutes more. Someone sent for a priest, and last rites were administered.

But Jack Slade was a stubborn man. He was tough and he was angry, and he was unwilling to die without getting revenge on the man who had bushwhacked him. The wounds certainly should have been fatal, but Slade simply refused to die.

The doctor worked on Slade for several hours. He poured a shot of whiskey down Slade's throat, then produced a slender knife from his satchel. He sliced off the vest and shirt Slade was wearing, then bent over one of the larger wounds. Carefully he inserted the point of the knife and began probing the wound.

Over the next several hours the doctor dug seven large shotgun pellets from Slade's body. The physician was also able to locate six other slugs which he could not get to; digging them out most certainly would have killed Slade. The physician later said a leather vest Slade had been wearing at the time of the shooting apparently stopped a lot of other buckshot and no doubt saved Slade's life. When the surgery was finally over it was almost midnight. The weary doctor told Ben Ficklin he could do nothing more for Slade. He also said he had no idea whether Slade would survive, that the wounds should have been fatal long ago, but Jack Slade appeared determined not to die. The only thing to do now, the doctor said, was wait.

The doctor warned Ficklin not to get his hopes up, however. He told Ficklin and a small crowd gathered outside the relay station that there still was not much hope. On the other hand, he conceded, Jack Slade was "one tough hombre."

Slade clung precariously to life. To everyone's surprise he made it through the night, and then through the next day, although he appeared to weaken. Those who saw him said Slade appeared to be in a coma. His breathing was shallow, his color ashen. But then, just when everyone thought they would soon be burying him, Jack Slade began to improve noticeably. After three days Slade had improved to the point at which the doctor decided he should be moved from Julesburg to a better medical facility somewhere else. Unfortunately, there were no better medical facilities anywhere in the West.

Slade was made as comfortable as possible under the circumstances and then was loaded aboard a special stagecoach headed east. Ben Ficklin ordered that his personal coach should carry Slade, although he privately admitted that he thought there was little chance the critically wounded man would make it as far as Omaha.

And so began one of the most incredible and difficult trips ever undertaken. Each day the stagecoach bounced and banged its way across forty miles or so of rutted dirt roads, through rivers and dry streambeds, over rocks and through gullies. Slowly and painfully it crossed the wide prairie, hour after agonizing hour. No one could do much to make it easier for the critically wounded Jack Slade, who clung tenaciously to life. When the coach hit a rut, everyone aboard was catapulted into the air, only to crash back onto the hard wooden benches a second later. With each bone-jarring jolt, Slade moaned and gasped for air. Every day, those accompanying Slade expected he would die. Each day Slade astounded everyone by clinging to life. Jack Slade simply refused to die!

Kansas City, although the largest "metropolis" west of the Mississippi, was hardly more than a cow town itself. Ficklin hoped he would find adequate medical facilities there, but he was bitterly disappointed. The town's doctors took a look at Slade and said there was nothing they could do. Grimly, Ficklin ordered Jack Slade loaded back onto the coach.

Eventually the gravely wounded gunslinger was taken all the way to Saint Louis—a distance of more than eight hundred miles from Julesburg—in search of medical help.[6] The trip took seventeen grueling days and must have been excruciatingly painful—but Slade hung on. Ficklin and others traveling with him claim that Slade never complained; the most they heard from the victim was the occasional involuntary moan when he was body-slammed by the rutted road.

The mere fact that Slade survived the grueling seventeen-day trip was amazing; his subsequent recovery from the gunshot wounds was absolutely miraculous. It was not, however, rapid. Jack Slade spent a full year at the hospital in Missouri before finally reaching the point where he could be released. Even then he was far from recovered. Doctors told Slade he would have to take it easy for years to come, and probably would never again handle hard horseback rides or heavy manual labor. Clearly these doctors did not know Jack Slade.

Slade snorted at the medical advice and told the doctors (and others) that nothing was going to keep him from going after the man who had shot him. And the day he was finally released from the hospital, Slade hobbled to the offices of the

Overland to report for work. Company officers were astounded and leery of Slade's physical capabilities—but they gave him a job in the warehouse.

Slade astounded everyone with his physical strength and his determination. From the first day he was hauling crates and hoisting heavy boxes onto freight wagons. Within a week, he was back astride a horse, and on his ninth day out of the hospital Slade bid his friends good-bye and headed West.

Some have suggested that the shooting temporarily turned Slade into a coward, and that when he returned to Julesburg he soon developed a reputation of being afraid now to face bad men. The book *The Hanging of Bad Jack Slade* states as a matter of fact that Slade became so docile upon his return to Julesburg that Ben Ficklin threatened to fire him unless he did something about growing crime in the area, and specifically about Jules Beni. Given Jack's personality and what factual information is known about him—before and after the shooting—that story seems far-fetched.

More likely are the other accounts of his return to Colorado. These stories (including old newspaper accounts) say that Slade returned to Julesburg fully intending to extract revenge from Beni. In fact, friends said that Slade was more determined than they had ever before seen him, that his eyes had taken on a strange, haunted look and that he was eager for a show-down with Jules Beni.

At the time of Slade's return to Julesburg, law-enforcement in the unsettled frontier West was a "sometimes" thing. Generally speaking, law enforcement was virtually non-existent in the sense that there was not a reliable, honest, nearby sheriff or United States marshal available whenever and wherever trouble reared its ugly head. Most communities simply had no law enforcement officers of any kind at all or had only one overworked deputy who covered thousands of square miles of land.

In most of the Colorado and Wyoming Territories, local citizens' groups frequently filled in the law enforcement gap themselves when things got so bad that something just had to be done. Citizens formed local vigilante groups that rounded up crooks (or suspected crooks), held an on-the-spot trial, and pronounced the suspect guilty (they were *always* found guilty). Then the convicted man was hanged from the nearest suitable tree or telegraph pole, and the trouble was over. For the moment.

Sometimes, though, the responsibility for law enforcement was turned over to the nearest local military commanders, providing one of the West's many army outposts was close enough. These army bases had originally been established to protect the settlers from Indian raids, and they still served as the only visible United States government authority in the region.

When Jack Slade left Saint Louis probably in late 1860 and headed back west, his first stop—before going to Julesburg, even—was at Fort Laramie, Wyoming. Fort Laramie was considered by most to be "the" law enforcement authority for all of Colorado, Wyoming, western Nebraska, and northwestern Kansas. Slade confided to friends that he wanted some responsible person to know that he was headed back to Julesburg and that he "anticipated difficulties should he encounter his old enemy, Jules Beni." In actual fact, Slade would have had it no other way. He planned to hunt down Beni and to kill him.

The military officers at Fort Laramie were well aware of the situation between Jack Slade and Jules Beni. They were also well aware of Jules Beni's reputation as a thief, a bully, a coward, and a bushwhacker. Like Ben Ficklin and a sizeable percentage of the general population, the military leaders at Fort Laramie believed that many of the robberies and horse thefts in northern Colorado, southeastern Wyoming, and the Nebraska panhandle were the work of Beni, and they were not prone to worry about Beni's health. In addition, Beni's bushwhacking of Jack Slade had been a cowardly act and a violation of The Code; there was hardly a man on the frontier who had any sympathy whatsoever for Jules Beni.

Although there are no written records to support the claim and the army itself always denied it, one of the highest-ranking officers at Fort Laramie is said to have told Jack Slade that the sooner he found and killed Beni, the better off everyone else would be. Another officer reportedly commented that there really could be no peace in the area until Jules Beni was dead.

Whatever was said and by whom, it is clear that by the time Slade left Fort Laramie for Julesburg, he had at least the tacit approval of the army for his deadly mission. That mission, of course, was to hunt down Jules Beni and extract revenge for the cold-blooded and cowardly attack Slade had suffered a year earlier. And whether army officers told Jack they approved of the killing or not, their subsequent actions make it clear they had no sympathy for Jules Beni. The implied approval was what Slade had hoped to hear when he went to Fort Laramie; now Slade wasted no time in taking advantage of the situation.

Even though Jules Beni had promised Ben Ficklin he would leave the area and never return, there is no evidence he ever intended to keep his word. Certainly Beni did not leave. In fact, he had little motive to do so. No one was actively hunting for him. The shooting of Jack Slade, reputed to be one of the toughest men ever to ride the Western trails, had earned for Beni a reputation that made most men think twice about crossing him. That's the sort of respect bullies love. When good men become cowards, thieves become rulers.

Additionally, Beni's well-being was directly tied to the region. He owned several ranches in northern Colorado and southern Wyoming, on which were housed sizeable herds of horses and cattle. The animals most likely were the ill-gotten result of rustling and theft from his old employer and from immigrants. Whenever he found a buyer for horses, Beni had only to ride to his nearest ranch, round-up one of the stolen herds and drive them to market. Then he could relax and live a life of luxury off the profits. And if he ran low on animals, Beni knew where to get more.

Within hours of riding out of Fort Laramie, Slade—accompanied by four of his most trusted associates—learned that Jules Beni was currently living somewhere along the Overland Trail, in the area between Julesburg and present-day Cheyenne. That's where Jack began his search. Some people believe that Beni was also simultaneously searching for Slade at this time—that he had somehow learned of Slade's return and guessed at his mission. There was at least a hint that Beni may have actually set out toward Julesburg for a classic showdown with Slade, although there is little actual evidence to support that rumor.

In the late afternoon, Slade and his four companions stopped to give their horses a drink of water at a Overland swing station located near the Nebraska-Colorado-Wyoming apex. To his delight, Slade learned that Beni had been at the same station just one hour earlier, and had left to continue his journey to Julesburg. Slade was still too sore from his gunshot wounds to push as hard as he once did, but wasn't about to miss this opportunity. He ordered his companions to ride on ahead of him in an effort to catch-up with and capture Beni, possibly at Bordeaux's ranch relay station on the North Platte (though this location would not have been en route to Julesburg).

One of the companions with Slade on this outing is believed to have been Hiram B. Kelly. Kelly was a close Slade ally at about this time, and—like most other men of the area—thought that as bad as he was, Slade did not deserve to have been bushwhacked. (Kelly later became a prominent southern Wyoming rancher and ultimately served as president of the Wyoming Stock Growers Association. Ironically, when he finally rose to that position of power and respect, Kelly denounced violent men like Jack Slade. He was a leader in a campaign for Wells Fargo to get rid of gunslingers, tough guys, and loners on its payroll. He argued that only by so doing could some semblance of law and order could come to Wyoming.)

Several hours after he and his friends parted, Slade rode into the Chansau Ranch relay station near the Colorado-Wyoming

border. There he was greeted with the news he had been waiting to hear. His friends had found and captured Jules Beni. To
the great delight of Jack Slade, Beni was at that very moment
tied to a rail in the corral behind this very relay station.

Slade dismounted somewhat stiffly and, according to witnesses, made a show of checking his Colt revolver. Satisfied
that the weapon was ready for use, he limped to the rear of the
station and finally confronted his old enemy.

Those who were present say that the moment was elec-
tric. Even tied to the post, Beni was defiant. He stared at
Slade though narrowed eyes, a grim look of determination on
his face.

Slade smiled slightly. Slowly—almost casually—he
strolled up to Beni and studied him silently for several long
seconds. Then without a word, Slade raised his revolver,
cocked it and fired—apparently intending to kill Beni. At the
last second, though, Beni jerked his head aside, and Slade's
bullet merely opened a sizeable gash along his cheek. (Some
writers have suggested that Slade deliberately "winged" Beni,
but that seems unlikely. Even a great shot would have difficulty opening a flesh wound in the face without fatally wounding
the victim.[7])

As Beni howled in pain and anger, Slade stood looking at
him quizzically. Then the old gunslinger appeared to have a
slight change of heart. Dropping his revolver back into its holster, Slade offered Beni an opportunity to write his last will and
testament, should he choose to do so. Slade said he thought it
only fair that a man go to his death having first made "appropriate preparations." Beni jumped at the opportunity.

Leaving one of his men to guard Beni, Slade walked back
to the relay station where a passing stagecoach had just
unloaded several passengers. Although the passengers were
chatting noisily as they stretched their legs after a long ride,
they fell silent as the leathery gunfighter walked into their
midst. Looking from face to face, Slade asked whether any of

the travelers knew how to write a will. One man allowed as how he could give it a try, and Slade bade the stranger to accompany him back outside.

Beni—struggling against the ropes and with blood pouring down his cheek—watched without a word as Slade and the stranger approached.

"Get talkin'," snarled Slade. "You got two minutes."

As the stranger began writing on a small pad of paper, Beni then dictated his will. (Unfortunately, there is no reliable record of what the will said.)

When Beni finished talking, Slade took the tablet. With a flourish, Slade signed the document as a witness, and invited the man who transcribed the will to do the same. Then Slade turned his back on Beni, and acting as if this was an everyday occurrence, indicated to the stranger to follow him back inside the station. When they entered the room, Slade invited the crowd to join him in a drink.[8] After the whiskey was poured Slade offered several toasts—to "honesty" and "fair play," and to "ridding the country of vermin."

Several drinks later, Slade re-emerged from the relay station. He walked slowly and somewhat unsteadily back to the spot where Beni was still tied to the gate post. Slade stood with a bottle of whiskey in his left hand and his revolver in the right.

As a small crowd watched in fascination, Slade took a long drag from the bottle, wiped his mouth with the back of his gun hand and then addressed the hapless Beni. Speaking in a low voice, Slade snarled, "Beni, now you're gonna pay for bushwhackin' me in Julesburg. We're gonna do this a little at a time, so that you'll know some of the pain you put me through in the last twelve months."

So saying, Slade took a step backward. He took careful aim and finally squeezed off a shot that tore a chunk out of Beni's right thigh.

Beni screamed in pain and questioned whether Slade's parents had been married. Slade just smiled. He took another long, slow drink of the whiskey and sighed deeply. Then Slade's eyes narrowed to mere slits. When he spoke again, he fairly hissed:

"Beni, I rode eight hundred miles in absolute misery, not knowin' from one minute to the next if I'd survive. Then I spent day after day, layin' in the hospital at Saint Louis, and every time I moved I hurt. My chest hurt, my arms hurt, my legs hurt, my head hurt. I was near dead and the doctors couldn't figure out why I didn't die.

"You wanna know why I lived, Beni? I'll tell you why. I lived for this moment. I lived for the day I would see you squirm, the day I would make you hurt as much as you hurt me. How does it feel, Beni? Are you hurtin' yet? Do you wish it was all over yet?"

Slade spit into the dirt and took another long drag from the bottle. "I used to wish it was all over, too, Beni, but I clung on. I was determined not to let it end. I've waited for this moment day and night for a more'n a year, Beni, and I aim to enjoy myself. Hope you're having a good time, too, you son of a bitch!"

(Several persons witnessed this soliloquy and while none recorded these exact words, most reported something similar to the amalgamated conversation related here.)

Slade cast an evil smile at the squirming Beni. Then raising the pistol again, Slade announced, "This one's going to be your left arm, Jules." His gently squeezed the trigger, and the bullet smashed Beni's upper left arm.

Over the next several hours Slade repeated the scene over and over again. Some accounts say Beni was shot at least twenty-two times over a period of twenty-four hours. Slade would appear at the corral, announce where he was about to shoot next, and then do so—taking out a chunk of muscle and skin and occasionally breaking a bone. Then Slade would take a long, satisfying swig from his whiskey bottle, make a few choice comments to Beni, and stagger back into the station to drink some more.

The stagecoach that had arrived just as the shooting start-ed was still at the station—passengers and crew alike unwilling to leave while the drama was being played out in the corral. Slade is said to have sometimes bought a round of drinks for the travelers gathered there, and on at least two occasions he is said to have remained inside the relay station for more than two hours at a time. Two more stagecoaches which normally would have quickly passed through the station during this time, stayed a full day in order to witness the slow killing of Jules Beni. There is no evidence any of the passengers or crew members objected to the way the execution was being carried out.

And after each round of drinks, Slade returned to the corral to resume slowly and painfully killing his old enemy. On each of these trips he was accompanied by several of the men who watched in horrified fascination at the grim drama unfolding before their eyes.

Several times during the long ordeal Beni lapsed into unconsciousness. Each time that happened, Slade went for a pail of water from the horse tank. Returning to his victim, Slade sloshed the cold water over Beni's head. Each time he did so, Beni regained consciousness.

At long last, though, Beni appeared ready to pass out for what could be the last time. Blood poured from wounds up and down his arms and legs and from the gaping wound on his cheek. He hung limply in the ropes and although his eyes were still open, they had taken on a decidedly glazed appearance. Beni now could do no more than manage an occasional mumbling curse at his tormentor, and not surprisingly some people question whether he remained coherent and aware of what was going on.

All at once Slade seemed to tire of the painful game. Onlookers said he muttered something they could not hear, then walked forward and shoved the barrel of the pistol into Beni's mouth. As the horrified witnesses watched, Slade fired one last shot. The bullet tore off half of Beni's head, bringing welcome death to the victim.[9]

Slade appeared unmoved by the bloody finish. Calmly he wiped the blood from the barrel of his revolver. Still standing in front of Beni's lifeless form, Slade casually reloaded his pistol and then dropped the weapon back into the holster.

After a moment, Slade produced his Bowie knife and slashed the ropes binding the dead man. Beni's body slid down the post and lay in a heap at Slade's feet. Kneeling beside his bloody victim, Slade neatly sliced off both of Beni's ears. Shoving the ears in his vest pocket, Slade picked up his whiskey bottle, raised it in a mock salute to Beni's body, then took another long drag. Smiling, he rose to his feet and stumbled back into the station.[10]

There are various accounts as to what Slade eventually did with the ears of Jules Beni. Almost all versions of the story say he wore at least one of the ears—either as a watch fob or on a chain around his neck—for the remainder of his life. He was said to be extremely fond of showing off this gruesome trophy each time he went on a drinking spree.

There is considerable dispute as to what happened to the other ear.

Many biographers say he also wore the second ear. A formal "state historical marker," erected by the State of Colorado at the site of the original Virginia Dale stagecoach station (on U.S. 287 about midway between Fort Collins, Colorado, and Laramie, Wyoming), says Slade nailed one of the ears to a post in the corral, presumably as a visible warning to anyone else who might consider crossing him. This information seems most likely to be accurate, as it was attested to by several of the stagecoach passengers.

A third story says Slade traded the second ear for a lifetime of free haircuts at a Julesburg barber shop.

A fourth story is that he carried both ears for a time, and then—when he was short on cash—traded the second ear for some whiskey money. This story, often repeated,[11] is probably not true. However, one newspaper writer of the day said that, "It is recounted that one of his favorite jests was to go into a saloon and buy a drink, then offer one of Jules' ears for payment."[12]

Another account of the ear incident is told in the excellent book, *An Ear in His Pocket*. In this version, Slade:

> ...pulled his knife from its scabbard and cut off at least one of Beni's ears, maybe both, depending on the historical source. Some accounts refute this and say Slade did not cut off either ear. There are numerous eye witness accounts, however, of a shriveled ear used later by Slade as a watch charm. One such account was by Thomas Bishop, a bull whacker on the old Mormon trail. He saw Slade entertaining the daughter of an emigrant who had stopped at Virginia Dale by putting a few pebbles in one of Beni's ears. He let the little girl play with it as a rattle. Bishop also said Slade always carried the ears with him and that one of his favorite jests was to enter a saloon and order a drink, then offer to pay the bartender with one of the ears.[13]

It is not surprising that a totally different story is told by Adeline Cayou Beni, the widow of Jules Beni. In fact, she told several versions of the Slade-Beni animosity. According to O'Dell and Jessen in their book, she claimed that the trouble between Slade and Beni started when Slade deliberately picked a fight with Beni in a bar. She says when Slade eventually went for his pistols, "...Jules was quicker with his shotgun and wounded Slade seriously."[14] She says Slade was taken to Denver for treatment of his wounds.

Somewhat later, she changed the story, saying the shooting occurred when a drunken Jack Slade went to Beni's home specifically to kill "a Frenchman." She claims that when Beni shot Slade in self-defense, Beni then offered to take Slade to Denver and pay all his doctor bills and other expenses if Jack would simply shake hands. She says Slade agreed, but after he got well decided to go back to Julesburg and kill Beni. In this version, she says Jack had a twenty-five-man posse that captured

Beni (who was by himself) and that they then tied him to a box. She says Slade fired several shots close to Beni, and that one of his pistol shots tore off an ear.

The widow Beni also told at least two other versions of the confrontation between Slade and Beni.

The morning after Beni was killed, Slade and his companions rode back to Fort Laramie, Wyoming, where Slade formally surrendered himself to the commanding officer. This happened to be the same officer who had advised Slade only a few days earlier that there could be no peace in the area until Beni was dead.

The officer went through the motions of taking Slade into custody, but after chatting with his subordinates decided that Slade had acted in accordance with the mysterious Code of the West, as a reasonable man was expected to do. The officer determined that no charges would be filed. To make it official, the officer wrote an official report, formally exonerating Slade.

Slade also wrote his own account of the incident and sent it off to his boss, company president and general supervisor Ben Ficklin. Ficklin exchanged a couple of letters with Slade and with the army at Fort Laramie, then he also exonerated Slade and welcomed him back as a full-time employee.

In truth, Ficklin and the Overland Company may have been extremely satisfied—even outright pleased—with the killing of Jules Beni. In the first place, his death actually did put an end to the series of robberies and horse thefts along the line. Although one can argue that the sudden stop in thievery could have been a mere coincidence, there is considerable evidence that Beni was deeply involved in the thefts.

More importantly, the story of Beni's spectacular killing spread like wildfire throughout the West. All at once, Jack Slade—whose reputation was somewhat tarnished after Beni bushwhacked him at Julesburg—was once again respected, and revered, and most importantly, feared—throughout the area. Robbers and horse thieves began to have serious second thoughts about any attack against the freight and stage company or any of its property. The mere reputation of Jack Slade as a cold, calculating killer did a great deal to protect the Overland and its employees. Robberies and horse thefts from the company came to a virtual stand-still.

_____

NOTES ON CHAPTER SIX

1. *Encyclopedia of Frontier Biography*, 1318.

2. There are numerous accounts of the shooting of Jack Slade, and no two of them are exactly alike. Some writers say Beni used a pistol in the shooting, some writers say it was a shotgun loaded with pistol balls, some say both a shotgun and a pistol were used. The version here seems to be the most widely accepted—and most logical—account of the incident. All writers agree in principle, however, that Slade was bushwhacked and that he was shot numerous times by Beni.

3. *History of Larimer County*, 1318.

4. *The Hanging of Bad Jack Slade*, 25.

5. *History of Larimer County*, 1318.

6. Other accounts have Slade recuperating in Denver or elsewhere.

7. Like everything else about the Jack Slade story, there is considerable debate over the exact location of the shooting. The *Encyclopedia of Frontier Biography*, 1318, says it occurred at the Cold Springs station, which was near present day Torrington, Wyoming.
   Several other historians identify this Cold Springs as being anywhere from forty to ninety miles south of Fort Laramie, but such a location would still make the shooting take place inside Wyoming. Since virtually all accounts agree that this shooting occurred in Colorado—the *Encyclopedia of Western Gunfighters*, 288–89 states it as a simple fact, as does the Colorado Historical Society—one assumes that there may have been another "Cold Springs," possibly in the general vicinity of Julesburg. (Locations with that name were common in the old West.)
   The *History of Larimer County* and *The History of Wyoming* both say Beni's shooting occurred at Chansau's Ranch, Colorado. These two books have proven accurate in other questionable areas, so one assumes this may be the correct location. To confuse the issue further, *The Hanging of Bad Jack Slade* claims the incident took place at Virginia Dale, northwest of Fort Collins. That information is certainly wrong, since Virginia Dale did not yet exist when Beni was killed. See also footnote 8.

8. *History of Larimer County*, 1319. Still another story says that Beni was captured while hiding on a ranch owned by Jack Slade, apparently waiting in ambush to kill Slade. This version says Beni was tied to a fence in front of Slade's ranch house and was killed at that point. Jay Robert Nash, *Bloodletters and Badmen* (New York: Warren Books, 1973), 342. This story is almost certainly an error. It seems likely that because the relay station where Beni was caught and executed was simultaneously a company relay station (supervised by Jack Slade) and a ranch house, the writer became confused.

9. The *History of Larimer County* records this version of the shooting, but says it is more likely that Slade wounded Beni with the first shot and killed him with the second immediately thereafter. Almost all other writers tell the story roughly as it is related here, although most admit that hard evidence to support any particular version is scarce. It is entirely possible that this is a highly "romanticized" version of what was a "simple" murder, carried out with one or two pistol shots.

10. Some accounts of this incident, including Mark Twain's, claim that the first wounding of Beni occurred late in the afternoon. Twain says "Slade examined Beni to make certain he could not escape and then retired for the night." Twain said the night was bitterly cold and Slade knew that Beni would suffer because of the cold. Twain also claims that during the lengthy multiple shooting the following day, Beni constantly begged to be killed. Then, says Twain, Slade personally led the burial party. *Roughing It*, 96.

Like so much of the remainder of the Jack Slade story, there are nearly as many differing accounts of the incident as there are persons who wrote of the incident. Even local newspapers at the time had widely different "facts." The account given here is the most commonly accepted version of the incident.

Many people believe Twain's version was never intended to be taken seriously; it was meant merely to be entertaining. His version of this incident written in 1870–72 and of Jack Slade himself appears based largely on a single trip he took through a portion of the area in 1861 and on reading he did in the ten years after that. It was also clear from his writings that Twain was enamored of Slade to the point where it may have colored his ability (or desire) to report factually on that portion of history. (Among other things, Mark Twain claimed that Jack Slade had already killed "at least twenty-six people"; most other historians say that at the time of Twain's journey to the area, Slade may have killed "only" twenty-two. We can document fifteen killings by Slade at this point in his life, although he was said to have also been involved in "several" undocumented killings while growing up. Ultimately, however, Slade probably killed a great deal more than twenty-six.)

There are many "eyewitness" accounts of the conversation between Slade and Beni during the killing. Probably most or all of them are entirely fictitious or at least greatly exaggerated. The version given here is an amalgamation of all such reports.

11. Kenneth Jessen, *Bizarre Colorado: A Legacy of Unusual Events and People* (Loveland, CO: J.V. Publications, 1994), 11.

12. *Encyclopedia of American Crime*, 664.

13. O'Dell and Jessen, *An Ear in His Pocket: The Life of Jack Slade* (Loveland, CO: J.V. Publications), 53.

14. *Ibid.*, 54–57.

CHAPTER SEVEN

GOOD GUY/BAD GUY

Throughout history, men have become famous erroneously or accidentally—after being credited for things with which they had nothing to do. Conversely, many men unknown to history actually molded key events by their little-known actions. Such a man was William Russell, co-owner of the Russell, Majors and Waddell Freight Company.

Clearly, Russell's company had much to do with settling the West, not only because of the men he hired, but because his company made it possible for settlers to acquire the supplies they needed to survive in the West. Beyond that, though, Russell almost single-handedly created the Pony Express. Although the Pony Express would change history and become an indelible part of American folklore, Russell's creation also left him bankrupt and led to his eventual demise.

The Pony Express grew out of intense competition between Russell, Majors and Waddell Company and its most bitter rival, the Butterfield Overland Mail Company. When Russell, Majors and Waddell bought the government contract to carry mail from Independence, Kansas, to Salt Lake City, Utah, Butterfield was getting lucrative (and unearned) government subsidies and government contracts offered in an effort to spur competition. Russell was infuriated at what he considered government favoritism and unfair competition. He set out for Washington, D.C., to demand changes.

In the winter of 1859, while in Washington, Russell met with California Senator William M. Gwin. Some sources say William F. Bee, who had strung telegraph wires from San Francisco to Sacramento, was also at that meeting. His interest was in establishing the fastest-possible communications between the western-most telegraph station in the Midwest (at Saint Joseph, Missouri) and the eastern-most station in California (Sacramento). Gwin proposed to Russell that he create the Pony Express, and promised if he did so, Gwin would do everything possible to win important government contracts and subsidies for Russell's freight company. Gwin admitted the Pony Express would probably be a money-losing proposition—but said if it survived just a year, he was certain he could win lucrative conventional mail contracts for Russell. He said he anticipated the Pony Express might lose a few "tens of thousands" of dollars in a year—but contracts awarded later would be measured in the "many hundreds of thousand of dollars."

Russell was excited at the challenge and opportunity. Although his company was already in financial trouble. Russell returned to Kansas City and convinced his reluctant partners, Alexander Majors and William Waddell, to spend $100,000 to get the Pony Express off the ground.

Unconfirmed reports indicate that Russell offered the manager's job for this new enterprise to Jack Slade, but that Slade wasn't interested. Neither, apparently, were Majors and Waddell, who thought Slade could not be spared from his duties on the freight line itself. Russell then began placing ads throughout the country, seeking brave (or brazen) young men as riders for this new service. An ad said to have been placed in a San Francisco newspaper read: "WANTED—young, skinny, wiry fellows, Not over eighteen. Must be expert riders, willing to risk death daily. Orphans preferred. Wages $25 per week." [1]

Perhaps it was a sign of the times that Russell was flooded with applications. Over a period of several weeks, he hired dozens of riders. Many of the riders were around twenty years

This illustration from Mark Twain's Roughing It *is captioned "The Superintendent as a Teacher" and shows an unnamed stage superintendent. Twain writes "when they [stage line superintendents] tried to teach a subordinate anything, that subordinate generally 'got it through his head.'"*

old; the youngest was eleven and the oldest about forty-five. Not many were orphans, but all were tough thrill seekers. Many of the men would later become famous in their own right.

One of the earliest hired was a young man named William Cody—known to his friends as "Billy." He was not yet known as Buffalo Bill—which is not terribly surprising; when he signed on as a rider, Cody was only fourteen years old! He would also soon become an enthusiastic admirer and supporter of Jack Slade.

Cody carried the mail for two months and then quit to help his ailing mother back in Kansas. But soon he longed to return to the frontier. Armed with a letter of introduction from Overland owner William Russell, young Cody went to Horseshoe Station to ask Jack Slade for a job:

> Almost the very first person I saw after dismounting from my horse was Slade. I walked up to him and presented Mr. Russell's letter, which he hastily opened and read. With a

sweeping glance of his eye he took my measure from head to floor, and then said:

"My boy, you are too young for a pony express-rider. It takes men for that business."

"I rode two months last year on Bill Trotter's division, sir, and filled the bill then; and I think I am better able to ride now," said I.

"What! are you the boy that was riding there, and was the youngest rider on the road?"

"I am the same boy," I replied, confident that everything was now all right for me.

"I have heard of you before. You are a year or so older now, and I think you can stand it. I'll give you a trail anyhow, and if you weaken you can come back to Horseshoe Station and tend stock."[2]

Young Billy Cody served Slade and the Pony Express well. Once he was reported to have ridden an additional eighty-five miles when he arrived at a station to find no one waiting to take the mochila on to the next station. The rider had been killed the day before. Cody rode on with the mail, and by the time he completed the round trip, he'd ridden 322 miles. Cody writes that soon:

> Slade heard of this feat of mine, and one day as he was passing on a coach he sang out to me. "My boy, you're a brick, and no mistake. That was a good run you made when you rode your own and Miller's routes, and I'll see that you get extra pay for it."
>
> Slade, although rough at times and always a dangerous character—having killed many a man—was always kind to me. During the two years that I worked for him as a pony express-rider and stage-driver, he never spoke an angry word to me.[3]

A few weeks later, Slade gave Cody a promotion of sorts, Cody writes:

> Slade, having taken a great fancy to me, said: "Billy, I want you to come down to my headquarters, and I'll make you a sort of supernumerary rider, and send you out only when it is necessary."
>
> ...During the winter of 1860 and the spring of 1861 I remained at Horseshoe, occasionally riding pony express and taking care of stock. [4]

While Bill Cody was boyishly enthusiastic in his praise of Slade, he was neither the only famous person to meet Slade, nor the only one to heap praise on the tough gunman.

During the same summer when Billy Cody was carrying the mail for Slade, another notable person, Mark Twain, met Jack Slade at Rocky Ridge Station. Twain writes about the encounter in his book *Roughing It*. He writes that Slade was:

> The most gentlemanly-appearing, quiet and affable officer we had yet found along the road... He was so friendly and so gentle-spoken that I warmed to him in spite of his awful history. It was hardly possible to realize that this pleasant person was the pitiless scourge of the outlaws, the raw-head-and-bloody-bones the nursing mothers of the mountains terrified their children with.
>
> The coffee ran out. At least it was reduced to one tin cupful and Slade was about to take it when he saw that my cup was empty. He politely offered to fill it, but although I wanted it, I politely declined. I was afraid he had not killed anybody that morning and might be needing a diversion. But still with firm politeness he insisted on filling my cup, and said I had traveled all night and better deserved it than he—and while he talked he placidly poured the fluid to the last drop. I thanked him and drank it, but it gave me no comfort, for I could not feel sure that he would not be sorry, presently, that he had given it away, and proceed to kill me to distract his thoughts from the loss. But nothing of the

True Williams drew many of the illustrations for Mark Twain's Roughing It *using detailed physical descriptions provided by Mark Twain, in consultation with his brother Orion Clemens. Many of the drawings closely resemble the actual people. It is not known if this is a close likeness of Jack Slade. Here Jack Slade, on left, pours coffee for Mark Twain.*

kind occurred. We left him with only 26 dead people to account for, and I felt a tranquil satisfaction in the thought that in so judiciously taking care of No. 1 at that breakfast-table, I had pleasantly escaped being No. 27. Slade came out to the coach and saw us off, first ordering certain rearrangements of the mail bags for our comfort, and then we took our leave of him, satisfied that we should hear of him again, someday, and wondering in what connection.[5]

While the boyish enthusiasm of Buffalo Bill Cody and Mark Twain resulted in clear exaggerations of Jack Slade, it remains one of the enigmas of the gunman that there were as many who adored him as there were who hated him. Interestingly, those who admired him almost always were portrayed as "the good guys," while his detractors were often on the other side of the fence.

In fact Slade himself contributed to the mixed reviews he got—by sometimes being gracious and big-hearted and heroic and at others being cruel and blood-thirsty. Mostly he was somewhere in between.

The story of the John Sarah family is a case in point. In the winter of 1861[6] a brutal, multiple killing made Slade famous —or infamous—throughout the land.

According to one version, the incident started on a cold November night when a Mexican-American and an Anglo-American, both employees of the U. S. Postal Service, got into a heated argument at a Russell, Majors and Waddell relay station known as La Bonte's Ranch. Eventually the dispute degenerated into gunplay, and when the smoke had cleared the Anglo was dead. The Mexican took refuge approximately thirty miles away at the Cottonwood Creek relay station, which doubled as a working ranch owned by John Sarah.

How Jack Slade got entangled in the dispute is open to conjecture. In the wide-open spaces of Wyoming there was little local law enforcement. Given Slade's personality, it requires no stretch of the imagination to guess that he had assumed the role of judge and jury. Perhaps the Anglo postal employee was a friend of his. It is known that shortly after the killing, Slade sent word to John Sarah that the Mexican was to leave the area immediately and to never return. Sarah apparently didn't take Slade's reputation seriously or was not frightened. At any rate, he told Slade to mind his own business. Sarah said that the Mexican was a paying guest at the ranch, and that so long as he paid his bills he was welcome to remain.

Slade was not a man to be told "no." A few nights after the rejection, Slade and a number of companions rode up to the Sarah Ranch. According to stories later told by Slade and his friends, John Sarah saw them coming, grabbed a rifle and began shooting. Slade and his companions shot back "in self-defense." In seconds, the ranch house was surrounded and scores of shots were fired into the building.

When the shooting finally stopped a short time later, John Sarah was dead. So, too, was Sarah's wife (a Lakota woman), another Lakota who was visiting the ranch, and a Frenchman by the name of Lonnel (presumably a guest). A young son of Sarah's survived the shooting.[7]

Another guest, a man named Frederick Winters, and two of Sarah's daughters who were carrying Sarah's newborn baby daughter had avoided the bullets by climbing out a back window and running out onto the prairie. They soon became separated, and Winters managed to work his way to safety. Eventually, Winters reported the incident to military authorities at Fort Laramie. He was not able to give any information on how the shooting started or who fired first. Once again there was insufficient evidence to bring charges against Slade. The military officials, who had absolute legal authority in the untamed West, ruled that Slade had been attempting to apprehend a killer, and that Sarah and the others had died while protecting that killer. No chargers were ever filed against Slade.

But some accounts of the incident indicate the story didn't end there. Sarah's three daughters who had raced out into the prairie in the tough Wyoming winter were found a few weeks later, frozen to death, a short distance from the ranch.[8] John Sarah's young son was found alive near the ranch buildings. Some accounts report that Jack and Virginia Slade raised this boy, and indeed, in some later periods of the Slades' lives a teenaged boy is reported to be living with them.

A narrative by Susan Bordeaux Bettelyoun, a mixed-blood Lakota woman, originally recorded in the 1930s and recently published for the first time, adds another perspective.[9]

Bettelyoun recalls that as a child, she remembers Jack Slade, whom she called "the notorious outlaw." She says that Slade and her father were good friends, although Slade frequently stole from her father.[10] She also tells a story that resembles the Sarah incident:

Slade had an Indian wife; in fact, he had been living with Indian women whom he bought in different places, but there were never any offspring from any of them. The last was a Sioux woman who was related to my mother. This woman had a brother staying with her; he had quite a large family. Slade was disappointed because his woman did not have any children. In a drunken state he got abusive. The brother tried to interfere and Slade shot him dead, also his wife and another. Four of the children ran away to the timber and froze to death that night. There was a five-year-old boy asleep at the time; this one Slade took with him.

He next married a Cherokee women who brought up the boy. The boy was called Mato Hinsma by the Sioux. He grew up. I never heard of him again after I came north.

However, Susan Bettelyoun, later corrected her account in a letter to the director of the Nebraska State Historical Society who was assisting her. She says she made an error, that the incident happened to a French trader, his Indian wife, and family, not within the family of Slade himself. Bettelyoun writes:

> I made a mistake in the Slade narrative. Slade came on the Platte in a drunk state at a white man's ranch above Fort Laramie on the Platte …In his drunken state he killed this white man. There were four or five children. It was midwinter and real cold. The wife, her brother, and four children ran away into the timber and all froze to death. There was only one boy left asleep in the bed. Slade took this boy and kept him. He took this boy to raise to his Cherokee wife.[11]

In addition, the book's footnotes cite another source about the incident. Quoting a document by Eli S. Ricker in the Nebraska archives, the notes offer this comparison:

> On the Bitter Cottonwood about twenty miles above [Fort] Laramie was a trading and mailing place and a stopping place for emigrants, log buildings here; was kept by a

Frenchman whom the Indians called Bare Bad Hair (Pehinsla Sica). His wife was an Indian. He and his wife and an Indian who was working for him were killed in the sixties by the Slade gang. Two or three of his children ran to escape; they found shelter in the brush and were frozen to death. It was winter.[12]

Whatever the details, it seems likely that Jack Slade was involved in the bloody killing of several people, some of whom were bystanders and others innocent children. And if indeed Slade adopted the surviving child, he must have once again felt remorse at the outcome of his actions.

The Bettelyoun book is the only known reference indicating that Jack Slade had Indian wives. It was not uncommon for white men on the frontier to maintain commonlaw relationships with Indian women. It also was not uncommon for traders, fur trappers, and other frontiersmen to "marry" several Indian women at the same time. Men like James Beckwourth —an infamous frontiersman, liar, horse thief, and trader—had several Indians wives at one time, not only to afford companionship but also to give him leverage in trading with various tribes.

However, Jack Slade was frequently praised for his complete and total loyalty to Maria Virginia Slade.

Notes on Chapter Seven

1. This advertisement is one of the most colorful images of the Pony Express, but some experts question its veracity. It is a part of the official history of the U. S. Postal Service and has been quoted in publications as respected as the *National Geographic* and the *Christian Science Monitor*. However, no actual copy of the ad survives and it appears not to have become part of Pony Express lore until about 1945. Online history of the National Oregon/California Trail Center (www.oregontrailcenter.org): *Orphans Preferred*, 252; and other sources.

2. *The Life of Buffalo Bill*, 104.

3. *The Life of Buffalo Bill,* 105.

4. *The Life of Buffalo Bill,* 110-118.

5. *Roughing It,* 96–97.

6. Various documents give the different locations and different dates for this killing. However, La Bonte's Ranch and John Sarah's Cottonwood relay station were located nearby Slade's Horseshoe Station headquarters in southeast Wyoming, and indicators point that the 1861 date is correct.

7. *Footprints on the Frontier,* 265. Again, it appears there is some confusion, mixing information from this incident and another that occurred somewhat later in Colorado. Ms. Trenholm claims that the surviving son of Sarah was adopted by Slade's wife and raised in Denver. We could find no other account that makes this claim, and it appears to be inaccurate. There was, however, an incident in which Slade apparently paid for the up-bringing of the son of one of his victims, but the incident is believed to have occurred several years later in Colorado. Like everything else about Jack Slade, unfortunately, there is some confusion as to the accuracy of many details.

8. *Footprints on the Frontier,* 265.

9. Susan Bordeaux Bettelyoun and Josephine Waggoner, Emily Levine, Ed., *With My Own Eyes* (Lincoln and London: University of Nebraska Press, 1998).

10. Susan Bordeaux Bettelyoun was born March 15, 1857, at Fort Laramie. Her father was James Bordeaux, the respected French American fur trader who later owned a trading post and road ranch near Fort Laramie. Her mother was Huntkalutawin, or Red Cormorant Woman, an honored woman in her band.

11. *With My Own Eyes,* 8.

12. *With My Own Eyes,* 131. This book's footnotes cite an interview of Eli S. Ricker by William Garnett on January 10, 1907, on file at the Nebraska State Historical Society archives.

CHAPTER EIGHT
THE IMPROBABLE RESCUE

T HE WORD WAS OUT. What the Cheyenne warriors had learned a few years earlier, thieves and rustlers learned now: both the Overland line and its chief "enforcer," Jack Slade, were just too tough to tangle with. Outlaws in the frontier West, who once considered stagecoaches, isolated relay stations, and freight wagons as easy pickin's, were left with only two choices. Most of them chose the easy decision by simply getting out of the area. New Mexico, Oklahoma and west Texas appeared to wind up getting most of these unwelcome characters.

A handful of gunmen and thieves, however, weren't smart enough to leave either Jack Slade or the stage and freight lines alone. These apparently thick-headed men decided to stay and fight it out—pitting themselves and their capabilities against Jack Slade. Some of them chose to challenge Slade himself to prove that they were as tough as he was. They virtually always came out second best in the inevitable confrontation. Other unsavory characters believed that the territory was so vast that there was no possible way Jack Slade could be everywhere at once. They chose to continue robbing and horse stealing from the tempting targets spread out along the Overland corridors. It was not a wise decision, and many men would wind up dead for having tried to outsmart, out-draw, or outrun Jack Slade.

One confrontation with hard-headed crooks, however, nearly cost Slade his life. Only the fact that he was married to an intelligent, quick-thinking, tough-acting woman kept him alive.

A gang of horse rustlers began targeting the stage line. They were especially after those relay stations along isolated stretches of the route in Wyoming. Over a period of several months the thieves made off with more than a hundred horses from a dozen relay stations.[1]

A part of the brazenness of these bandits probably was the outgrowth of the fact that for some time no one seemed to be searching for them. Almost no local law enforcement existed along the trail itself. The army was preoccupied with Indian raids and the looming Civil War, and Jack Slade was late getting on their trail because of preoccupation with some strictly personal matters. The badman had acquired a wife, Maria Virginia, prior to this incident although no documents exist to verify the exact date of his marriage.

When Jack finally returned to work, his first order of business was to stop the horse thefts from relay stations west of present-day Laramie. Ben Ficklin wrote to Slade that the thieves were costing the company more than it could afford to lose and placed the "highest priority" on finding and stopping the horse rustlers. Slade, who never liked working with any more men than absolutely necessary, rounded up three of his most trusted friends and set out for Julesburg, which would be the starting point of his search.

Slade knew that the thieves were somewhere in southeastern Wyoming, and that they would not be far off the stage route. Beginning at Julesburg, Slade and his companions mapped a trail toward Fort Laramie. Along the way they stopped at each relay station and ranch house, asking questions.

After talking with several stationmasters and ranchers near the Wyoming border, Slade concluded that a gang of six men were involved in the horse thievery. From two stationmasters who had been the victims of horse stealing, he also obtained fairly good descriptions of several of the men. Just seventy-two hours after being his search, Slade knew he was already getting close. Following the trail of the outlaws toward present-day Cheyenne, Slade learned that men answering the description of the horse thieves had been seen heading west from there a short time earlier. Slade followed the suspects.

When he arrived at a road ranch near present-day Laramie in the late afternoon of the third day, Slade learned that his suspects had departed less than two hours earlier. Witnesses said the rustlers had ridden toward the southwest. This time of year the suspects couldn't go very far in that direction; a tall mountain range lay just a few miles in that direction and the mountains were impassable because of deep snow. These facts indicated that the rustlers had a camp not far away—possibly on the flat lands near where Woods Landing is now located. Ironically, that would be within twenty-five miles of Virginia Dale. Slade's little posse hastened on, hoping to catch the gang by nightfall. They were rewarded a short time later when they picked up the trail of a half-dozen horses, moving toward the foothills. Slade felt confident that he was getting very close to his prey.

Shortly before dark, the trail passed through a low meadow at the foot of the Rockies. Beavers had dammed the little stream in the valley, turning the area into a shallow, muddy swamp. After the tracks entered the marsh, Slade lost the trail.

Angry at this turn of events and the possibility the suspects might get away during the night, Slade ordered his men to split up and fan out. They were to search the parameters of the marsh for any sign of the suspects. Whichever man picked up the trail first was to ride back to the starting point, then fire his gun three times to alert the others. Although the gunshots would alert the bandits that someone was in the area, Slade hoped that if the shots were fired near the main trail the bandits might think it was merely a hunter and would not become alarmed enough to break camp and leave the area.

The marsh turned out to be considerably larger than Slade expected. Within a short time Slade and his three companions were widely separated.

Slade was riding alone and was apparently some distance from any of his friends, peering at the ground, searching for signs left by the suspects. He stopped every few minutes and studied the terrain, looking for hoofprints, broken twigs, or other indications that he was on the right trail. Slowly crossing through an area thick with heavy underbrush, Slade suddenly found himself staring down the business end of three rifles. There was no chance to go for his weapon; Slade was a prisoner of the men he had been hunting! Cursing himself for his carelessness, Slade was led to the rustlers' camp.

The horse thieves recognized Slade at once. They would have been elated to have captured a pursuer under any circumstances, but when that pursuer turned out to be the famous gunman Jack Slade the rustlers were nearly giddy with delight. Sneering at Slade, the leader warned that if he cried out or tried to escape, they would shoot him without hesitation. Slade knew that in spite of their brave front, his captors were nervous—and that nervousness might cause them to shoot him accidentally. Slade went to great lengths to appear to cooperate. He allowed himself to be disarmed and led away, bound hand and foot.

Since no one was around when Slade was captured, the three bandits assumed that he was alone. In fact, there is no information as to where Slade's friends went or why they never came to rescue him. The thieves led Slade to a small clearing where the other three horse thieves were waiting. The six bandits rejoiced at their great luck, having captured Jack Slade. They ridiculed Slade for coming after them without any help, and for stumbling blindly into their midst. Didn't he realize they would be watching for someone trailing them? Didn't he think they were smart enough to split up and lie in wait to make certain they hadn't been followed? How foolish Slade was! After several minutes of taunting Slade, the thieves took him to a small log cabin hidden in a remote box canyon two miles from the point where they'd captured him.

As time wore on, the rustlers became more and more abusive. Soon they were not satisfied just to taunt or demean Slade. Since the prisoner was securely bound, they seized the opportunity to rough up Slade a bit. One of the bandits told Slade that this corporal punishment was in retaliation for Slade's hanging of a friend of theirs, another horse thief, two years earlier. The physical abuse was not severe—but it also was not very smart. Slade gritted his teeth and bore the assault, but already he was looking for an opportunity to get away— and get even.

Eventually Slade was taken inside the cabin, where he was tied to a chair. He was placed in the middle of an otherwise bare room, and the cabin's windows were shuttered. For a time it appeared the men would make good on their threat to shoot Slade at any moment, but eventually greed began to work on the minds of the rustlers. Soon the captors were debating whether to hold Slade for a ransom and how much he might be worth. At least two members of the gang proposed that stage line owners Russell, Majors and Waddell might willingly pay a healthy ransom to save the life of Slade, to whom they owed a great deal. The debate raged for some time before the thieves decided that asking for a ransom was too risky. Instead the gang agreed they should simply shoot Slade and get it over with.

Slade received the news calmly. He told the rustlers that he wasn't afraid to die but asked if his executioners would grant him one last request. He appealed to them as gentlemen to permit him one final meeting with his bride. He reminded the thieves that he was tied up and under armed guard, and that he could do nothing to harm them. On the other hand, he felt that as honorable men they would permit him a final farewell.

Slade's appeal put the bandits on the spot. The six bandits went off to a corner of the room and talked in hushed tones. After several minutes the leader announced that they had decided to permit Slade's wish for one final visit with Virginia. They warned Slade that they would be on their guard, that one wrong move would cost the lives of both Slade and his wife. At that, one of the bandits was sent to fetch Virginia Slade.

When one of the gunman arrived at Slade's home the following morning, Virginia was stunned by the news that her husband was being held prisoner and was about to be executed. To her credit, however, she neither argued nor hesitated. Virginia was eager to see her husband one last time before he was killed. Within minutes, Virginia and her gunman escort were back on the trail toward the cabin.

Arriving at the cabin, Virginia dismounted before the watchful eyes of her husband's kidnappers. The leader of the gang stepped forward, halted Virginia, and started to frisk her. She was indignant and threatened to slap him. She chastised him roundly, saying that only a scoundrel of the worst kind would suggest that a lady who was about to become a widow would risk a final meeting with her husband by concealing a weapon. And no gentleman, she said, would ever physically touch a woman already in mourning.

The man appeared startled by this emotional outburst and took a couple of steps backward. He nodded at his companions and they also backed away. Without further ado Virginia was permitted to go inside the cabin and be alone with her husband. Four of the bandits stood around watching, probably congratulating themselves for being such gentlemen; the other two men accompanied Mrs. Slade.

With tears streaming down her face, Virginia was led inside the cabin. After a few moments, she turned to the nearby gunmen and scolded them severely for standing so close while she spent her final minutes with her husband. Speaking angrily through her tears, Virginia demanded that she be left alone for a few moments while she and Jack said their final good-byes and she regained her composure.

The bandits apparently were surprised at the tongue lashing and backed quickly toward the door. After a moment's hesitation they stepped outside the cabin to permit the grief-stricken couple their last few seconds together.

The thieves may have been gentlemen, but Virginia felt no compunction to be a lady. Once alone with her husband, she quickly produced two revolvers which she had secreted beneath her skirt. She also produced a Bowie knife, with which she slashed the ropes binding Jack to a chair. Then with each of them holding a pistol, Jack kicked open the door, and they dashed from the shack, guns blazing.

The startled thieves scrambled for cover, and in the confusion of the moment Jack and Virginia reached their horses. In a flash, both were mounted and lashing their horses to race from the box canyon. They escaped totally unscathed.

Jack knew that with winter snows on the ground, there was no easy route for the rustlers to escape; their only practical exit from the area was back along the trail they come on. Slade escorted Virginia to safety, then quickly rounded up a posse and headed back toward the cabin. It took only minutes to pick up the trail of the fleeing bandits. In spite of the deep snow, they had set out in a north by northwest direction parallel to the mountains. (There is no indication whether the other three "trusted" members of Slade's original posse were a part of the new posse.)

The horse thieves were running for their lives and managed to cover considerable distance in the time it took Slade to organize a posse and return to the chase. By the time Slade began to gain on them they were already moving deep into the mountains. The rustlers probably hoped Slade would be less speedy in taking up their pursuit and fall farther behind them. Their hope failed to take into consideration Slade's reputation, or the likelihood that he would be eager to take revenge against men who had captured and mistreated him.

For three days the outlaws raced ahead of Slade, driving their horses up steep, rocky mountainsides, across snowy valleys and back down again, endlessly pushing onward across the rough terrain. Slade and his posse moved as quickly as they could in pursuit of the thieves. The deep snow made it generally easy to follow the trail and—as anyone who has ever ridden through the snow knows—it is much quicker to follow than to lead.

Slade pushed as hard and fast as he could. Two horses in the posse went lame and the men dropped out of the chase, but Slade drove the others harder and harder. Slade and ten other men relentlessly continued their dogged pursuit and slowly gained ground on the thieves.

Shortly after noon on the third day of the chase, the posse got close enough to actually see the thieves about two miles ahead of them. The thieves saw the posse at the same time and tried to move their exhausted horses more quickly. By that time, men and animals on both sides were worn out and the "chase" had slowed to a walk. Now, however, Slade had the hated enemy in sight, and he seemed regenerated by the thought that they soon would be his. He urged his companions to hurry.

Among the six rustlers there were now early indications of panic. One of the thieves began talking about surrendering. At first, his companions would hear nothing of it, but as the day wore on and it became clear that the posse was relentless in their pursuit, others began making the same suggestion. Eventually the gang concluded that it was simply useless to run any farther. Besides, they believed, if they surrendered peacefully there was at least a possibility they would be allowed to live—perhaps the posse included some men who would argue against lynching. Clearly these rustlers didn't know how Jack Slade operated.

Standing on a ridge in plain view, the six horse thieves dismounted. They laid down their rifles and unbuckled their gun belts so that their six-guns slid to the ground. Then all six men stood with their hands raised high in the air.

It took several minutes for the weary posse to reach the surrendering bandits. When they finally rode up to the spot, everyone was too tired to even speak or move. Everyone, that is, except Jack Slade.

Slade slid from the saddle and walked to the six weary bandits, who stood side by side. Slade walked along the line, inches from the men, staring into their faces. At last he found what he was looking for. Recognizing the one who had beat him during the time he was prisoner, Slade put his face nearly against that of his tormentor. Without a word, Slade pulled his pistol and shot the man in the chest.

A look of absolute surprise froze on the victim's face, and he stood motionless for a long second before tumbling to the ground dead. The other five thieves watched, presumably in terror.

Dropping the smoking revolver back into its holster, Slade turned toward the posse. With a nod toward the remaining thieves he said simply, "Hang 'em."

The five rustlers were led to a pair of trees a short distance away. Slade watched without visible emotion as the posse tied nooses and placed one over the neck of each man. The other end of the ropes were looped across a low-hanging branch, then the men were helped onto their horses. At last, all five were ready. One of the kidnappers began sobbing and pleaded for his life—but Slade appeared not to hear.

Walking to the rear of the horses, Slade drew his revolver and fired one shot into the air. The startled animals bolted in fright and raced away, literally running out from under the thieves. All five kicked and twisted in the air for several minutes.

The posse watched quietly, each man left to his own thoughts, as the struggling and squirming slowly diminished. At last, the final victim quit moving. The five bodies hung limply, swaying gently in the mountain breeze. Without a word, Slade climbed back into the saddle, laid the reins across his horse's neck and turned back down the trail.

Somewhat later, Slade said to several friends that it was too bad the hangings had to take place in such an isolated spot. He said he would have preferred to hang the victims along a heavily-traveled trail where the bodies would have served as a warning to other thieves.[2]

As it turned out, Slade's preference for a public display of the hanging victims was not necessary. The possemen who had been with Slade told the story over and over—told how Slade had appeared emotionless as he shot the leader and hanged the others. The story was usually told in hushed tones and was frequently accompanied by a shudder. Men shook their heads knowingly, and the next time they saw Slade coming they were likely to cross the street.

Soon the story spread throughout the territory. Many people were shocked—and most were thoroughly impressed—with Slade's cold efficiency. Who knows how many horses were *not* stolen and how many stagecoaches were *not* robbed thereafter as a result of would-be thieves hearing how Slade dealt with their predecessors?

But it wasn't only the local citizens and thieves who heard about the hangings; that story and others like it soon were being told as far east as Saint Louis. It is said that each time Overland supervisor Ben Ficklin heard about another shooting or hanging orchestrated or personally carried out by Jack Slade, Ficklin simply smiled.

"Every time he hangs another man, we accomplish two things," Ficklin once told a co-worker. "We get rid of another outlaw, and Slade's reputation increases another notch. That means some other horse thief leaves the territory!"

In fact, Slade's behavior and his "no nonsense" reputation were so effective that many other frontier businesses decided to try the same tactic. Ranchers and other freight companies were soon making it a habit to hire tough, mean-spirited gunfighters to protect themselves from armed robbers or Indian raiders. They actually encouraged these hired guns to hang a suspect or two so that their reputation would spread just as Jack Slade's had done.

Not all of the Overland Stagecoaches were as elaborate as this one, nor were most pulled by a team of all-white horses. This photograph probably was made shortly after Slade left for Montana. (Courtesy Western History Collection, Denver Public Library)

Somewhat surprisingly, the tactic worked! Having a well-known, cold-blooded killer as your personal "enforcer" proved effective time after time:

> Western express companies responded to [robberies of their wagons] by organization of private protective forces. Different conditions required unusual means of commercial response. When the Army failed to protect the Butterfield Line in Texas, the company hired as drivers such personalities as William A. 'Big Foot' Wallace, and sometimes assigned several armed riders as escorts. The Overland Express obtained the services of the notorious Joseph A. 'Jack' Slade as supervisor of its vast district extending from Missouri to Utah. With no special legal authority he exercised great power... Slade maintained a kind of order along the line from 1859 to 1863.[3]

Law-abiding citizens weren't excited about having gunmen hanging around their towns, but if the hired guns left them alone, few complained. The truth was that hiring known gunslingers and even known outlaws to guard their property made good sense to the wagon companies and ranchers. The result was fewer robberies, less horse rustling, and less crime in general.

Even the army soon believed that having men like Jack Slade around was not a bad practice. As the Civil War escalated, the army was too busy fighting and trying to deal with the Indians to take on the added burden of protecting travelers and ranchers from armed robbers and rustlers. As a result, the army rarely took action against these hired guns if their killings in any way seemed just. Local law enforcement officers also looked the other way as increasing numbers of private guards hanged, shot, or chased away troublemakers and thieves. And if they occasionally hanged the wrong man by mistake, who was to know?

Horse thievery was a major frontier problem in the middle and latter 1800s, and the unwritten code of the mostly lawless West demanded that the thieves be found and hanged on the spot. If they were caught and executed by these private guards, fewer questions were raised, less of the taxpayers' money was spent, and fewer crimes were committed.

Some less hardened settlers who wished the West was a little more law-abiding and sophisticated plus a handful of other reformers sometimes suggested that the rustlers should at least be given a trial before they were hung. The fact was, however, that judges and courts were scarce, victims of rustling or hold-ups were impatient, and trials were time-consuming and costly. The vast majority of the Western population apparently favored the more direct approach. Lynching a thief from the nearest tree meant never having to worry about recidivism. It would be another full decade before courts and judges and trials became common in Colorado and Wyoming—even longer in the Utah and New Mexico Territories.

In the wake of this new attitude, even Jack Slade's embarrassing little "indiscretions"—shootings or hangings that apparently occurred only because he had been drinking and not because he was punishing a horse thief—drew little attention from either company officials or area lawmen. Most of the men who ran afoul of Jack Slade's indignation, after all, were low-lifes and ne'er-do-wells, who hung around saloons with unsavory companions. Frontier citizens felt the territory was better off without them, regardless of how they met their demise.

But, alas! Public opinion is fickle, and some of that "boys will be boys" attitude began to erode as Jack Slade's "indiscretions" became more and more common over the passing months and years. Jack's always unstable personality now became a full-blown Dr. Jekyll and Mr. Hyde syndrome; he could be a model citizen or he could be an insane, trigger-happy killer. A citizen never knew what he was going to get.

Some writers of the era quote friends and acquaintances of Slade's as saying he was "…a fine, docile and decent man when sober, but a cold killer, meaner than a skunk, when drinking." And with passing time it was increasingly difficult to find Slade when he was entirely sober, kind or gentle.

In 1860, for example, Slade was drinking at a saloon in northeastern Colorado, possibly in Julesburg. Sometime earlier Slade had exchanged heated words with the bartender. Now as he sat drinking Slade became increasingly angry.

Slade asked for another brandy, and the saloon-keeper reached under the bar. It's not clear whether Slade thought the bartender was reaching for a weapon, or simply that he was reaching for the cheaper brandy which was kept under the bar. Whatever his thinking, Slade clearly did not like what was going on.

"There'll be none of that," Slade snapped. "Get me the good stuff."

The bartender did not protest, but, according to witnesses, he turned around and reached for a bottle on a shelf behind the bar. As he did so, Slade whipped out his revolver and shot the bartender in the back. The victim died within a few minutes.

Slade watched without apparent emotion as a nervous barroom crowd gathered around the body. Without ever speaking, Slade eventually turned and casually strolled out of the tavern. No one ever challenged him about the shooting, and no warrant was ever issued for his arrest in connection with the killing.[4] Why he escaped the wrath of the law is not entirely clear, except that lawmen were scarce and most men by this time were afraid of tangling with Slade. Unfortunately, Jack's darker side seemed to feed on this absence of penalty.

Not long after the barroom shooting, Slade spent an hour or so imbibing at another bar in Julesburg, then stepped outside "for a breath of air." Outside the bar he sat down in a wooden chair and leaned back against the tavern wall. Several of Slade's most frequent companions joined him there, engaging in small talk.

Suddenly Slade sat upright, leaning forward in the chair. Across the street, walking toward him, was a man whom Slade had frequently called a horse thief. On two earlier occasions, Slade had tried to track down the suspect, but was never able to find him.

Presumably, the suspected horse thief knew that Slade was after him. Why he ventured into Julesburg—Slade's increasingly favorite hangout—is anybody's guess. Perhaps he believed he would be safe in front of witnesses, or maybe he didn't understand how Slade operated. There's even a chance that he wasn't aware that Slade was in the area, although with a key Overland home station in the community, that seems unlikely. Whatever the reason, the suspected horse stealer was now ambling along the dusty street apparently unaware that he was walking directly toward Jack Slade.

"Gentleman, that man's a thief," said Slade as he drew his Colt revolver. "As you can see, he is a good twenty yards away. I shall clip the third button on his vest." Slade took careful aim and squeezed off a shot. The bullet smashed through the third button and shattered the victim's heart.

Slade is said to have calmly reloaded the revolver and dropped it back into his holster without so much as casting a glance toward the victim, now lying in the street. Turning to his companions as he arose from the chair Slade apologized for creating work for them—but invited them to join him in burying the victim. They all did so.[5]

These and other incidents involving Slade continued to have the desired effect for the Overland Company. The outlaws roaming the Colorado Territory and adjacent areas of Kansas, Nebraska, and Wyoming did their best to stay away from Jack Slade.

In fact, Slade was so effective at what he did that he nearly put himself out of work. By the end of 1861, serious problems in the Sweetwater Division—which was Slade's territory and Slade's responsibility—had virtually ceased to exist. The outlaws had all moved a little further west or south.

Fortunately for Jack, about this time the Overland Stage Company purchased Wells Fargo's freight franchises along the front range of the Rockies and began reorganizing the stage and freight line into a more efficient operation. Among the first major actions of the new owners was to open an important new stage route from Denver to near present-day Laramie, Wyoming. This key connecting artery ran along the eastern face of the Rocky Mountains, roughly along the famous Old Cherokee Trail. The new route, known as the Overland Trail West, passed through territory that until this time was largely uninhabited by white men. This was Indian hunting ground, although the Indians who occupied the territory—Arapahos, mostly, and a few Southern Cheyennes—were generally considered friendly to whites. Slade began to help establish the new route.

There were, however, two other serious problems along this new stretch of trail. First, many of the outlaws Jack Slade had earlier chased from the Sweetwater Division now resided in the newly opened territory. Among this group was L.H. "Lefty" Musgrove, who was running the largest cattle rustling ring in

The Overland station at LaPorte, Colorado, was once shot up by an angry Jack Slade. (Courtesy Fort Collins Public Library)

the country. Musgrove had thieves working in eight western states and territories, all of them directed from his headquarters at Livermore, Colorado.

It is probably significant and certainly an indication of Jack Slade's reputation, that Musgrove—who considered himself a great gunfighter—carefully avoided any confrontation with Jack Slade. There are reports that when drinking, Musgrove frequently boasted to companions that he could out-shoot Slade anytime he wanted to—but although the men lived only a few miles apart at times, no "opportunity" ever presented itself. Additionally, Musgrove is reported to have quietly instructed his thieving minions to always avoid Overland Company livestock.

The company was aware that this new route was literally crawling with rustlers, robbers, and gunmen. Something would have to be done to control them. But thieves were only a part of the difficulty.

The second problem was that establishing the new trail required building a series of swing and home stations, recruiting help and generally organizing a bunch of rough and tumble cowboys into obedient, trustworthy, and hard-working employees. It was not a job that most men would even attempt.

Who better to handle such a nearly-impossible assignment than Jack Slade? In early 1862, Slade was transferred from the Sweetwater Division of the old Northern Route of the Overland to temporary headquarters at LaPorte, Colorado, on the north bank of the Cache La Poudre River in Larimer County. From there, he began recruiting workers to begin construction on a series of relay stations. At the same time Slade was actively pursuing his other assignment—a relentless campaign against horse thieves and outlaws in the area.

Given Jack Slade's past accomplishments, one might have anticipated that the gearing-up for the new route would go exceedingly well. Jack did not disappoint his employers. Perhaps it was Slade's efficient management or because local residents wanted to encourage stage service in the area, or even possibly because of Slade's reputation with a gun. Whatever their reason, construction of the new stations went quickly and smoothly.

Some of the cooperation Slade enjoyed may also have been at least partially the result of the ever-present reminder offered by the shriveled ear that dangled from Slade's watch fob—the ear of Jules Beni. Slade wore the ear continuously and loved to show it off. The conspicuous fob was a powerful reminder of the kind of man who was in charge of these operations.

The new Overland Trail West opened well ahead of schedule after encountering a minimum of problems. The ease with which the project was completed should have raised questions in someone's mind; it was the almost predictable lull in the storm that was Jack Slade's life.

NOTES ON CHAPTER EIGHT

1. Though this incident is widely reported, the date and exact location differ in different sources. Obviously it was after Jack and Virginia were

married. Some versions place it near Laramie City, so perhaps it was after they established Virginia Dale in 1862.

Since it seems unlikely that there was a settlement at Laramie City during the approximate time frame of the confrontation, another possibility is that the incident took place near the mountains west of *Fort* Laramie rather than at Laramie City. Time seems to have blurred the identity of the setting.

2. This is the one Jack Slade story on which virtually all historians agree. Based on information taken from the Colorado Historical Society Museum and Library, Denver, Colorado.

3. Frank Richard Prassel, *The Western Peace Officer* (Norman, OK: University of Oklahoma Press, 1972), 136–37.

4. *Encyclopedia of Western Gunfighters*, 286.

5. *Roughing It*, 64. Twain has the incident occurring at the Rocky Ridge station in Wyoming.

CHAPTER NINE

DEMON RUM

A BOUT THIS TIME, Jack Slade seemed to get bored with life. He had established the Overland route from Denver to Fort Bridger in record time and with few problems. The bad news was that once that challenge ended, Jack Slade's personality began to deteriorate again, and his mood seemed to sink lower than ever before. Over the eighteen months between the middle of 1862 and late in 1863, Jack Slade's troubled and growing schizophrenia became more and more apparent.

His work on behalf of the Overland Stage Company continued to be exemplary. When he was on the job there simply was no better employee. He supervised the company's most efficient and smooth-running district. Slade and his employees kept stagecoaches and freight wagons moving quickly, on-schedule, and virtually trouble-free along the new Overland Trail West. Few bandits or horse rustlers caused confrontations, and from a business standpoint, things were going very well.

By this time, Slade's name was probably the most recognized on the frontier, at least in terms of "enforcers" or gunmen. It had even begun appearing regularly in the pulp newspaper and magazine trade in New York, and Mark Twain had published his first accounts of meeting this famous gunslinger.

Those who liked Slade called him by one of several names; Virginia Trenholm in her history says that folks in Wyoming called Slade "Alf," a shortening of his middle name. Among

The Virginia Dale relay station near the Wyoming State Line in northern Colorado where Jack and Virginia lived. This photograph, probably taken about 1900, indicates the shape and size of the building during Jack's tenure as supervisor of the stagecoach line. (Courtesy Western History Collection, Denver Public Library)

fellow employees from St. Louis to Salt Lake City, and among the general public who admired or respected him, though, "... He was variously known as 'Jack' Slade, or 'Cap' Slade—but in the days when he really achieved fame he was known as 'Slade of the Overland'!"

In spite of Jack's fearsome reputation, he had a lot of fans and supporters. Many people thought exactly what was needed—both by the freight line and by law-abiding citizens who yearned for someone to call upon to control a generally lawless crowd of drifters—were men like Slade. In many respects, Jack Slade was not unlike Wyatt Earp or Bat Masterson or many of the other famous sometimes-lawmen of the old West. For the most part, these men switched back and forth between roles as lawmen and roles on the questionable side of the law. Slade was neither robber nor thief, but he certainly was on the wrong side of the law in terms of many of the killings attributed to him. But, like Earp and Masterson and Hickok and the others, Slade was completely effective in dealing not only with thieves and rustlers he was hired to control, but also with hard-nosed teamsters and other freight line employees as well:

> It was perhaps the hard reputation he bore that made him a good man for this job. The hardy teamsters who drove the Overland coaches were not, by any stretch of the imagination, milksops. They were, to put it bluntly, tough men and wild, and it took a strong man and a rough one to be their boss.
>
> Whatever else may have been said of Slade, he got his coaches through despite Indians, highwaymen, or drivers, and his name was a terror across Colorado and the West.[1]

During the time he was building the new stage line, Slade had selected a beautiful mountain setting about twelve miles south of the Wyoming border to serve as his permanent home as well as a key home station along the new Overland Trail West. He named the new station in honor of his wife—Virginia Dale—and the station quickly became a centerpiece for the line and an attraction to northern Colorado travelers.

There is no question the mountain setting was beautiful. Samuel Bowles, a Massachusetts newspaper editor traveling the line, wrote of the new station:

> Virginia Dale deserves its pretty name. A pearly, lovely-looking stream runs through a beautiful basin of perhaps one hundred acres, among the mountains… stretching away in smooth and rising pasture to nooks and crannies of the wooded range; fronted by rock embankment, and flanked by the snowy peaks themselves. It is difficult to imagine a more loveable spot in Nature's kingdom.[2]

But it wasn't just the little dale itself that was so beautiful; the surrounding mountain peaks were awe-inspiring, and local folklore made them even more interesting and beautiful. To the west were heavily-wooded mountains filled with deer, bears, mountain lions, and elk.

Just east of Virginia Dale was a tall hill, sloped on one approach, but ending in a sheer drop of several hundred feet on the other. The cliff was called "Lover's Leap." Local residents claimed it was the spot where two young Indian lovers—one Arapaho and one Cheyenne—leaped to their deaths because custom prohibited them from marrying one another.[3]

Just south of Virginia Dale were several tall mesas where Indians still chased stampeding buffalo herds. In their panic the animals would dash off the face of a cliff and tumble to their deaths below. In that killing ground, the Indian women butchered the animals, taking meat and skins for use by the tribe.

While the Virginia Dale station was under construction, Slade posted armed guards on a third high hill which lay just to the east of the station. These Slade sentinels were there to watch for trouble from bands of renegade Indians, horse thieves, or armed robbers.

Southeast of this hill was a fourth towering mountain peak. From the upper reaches of this mountain a man could enjoy an excellent view of the Overland Trail for many miles in both directions. A man standing on a boulder at the western edge of the highest ridge would know thirty to forty-five minutes in advance if a stagecoach or freight wagon was coming from either direction along the trail. Unfortunately, the strategic value of this mountain was known throughout the area to both law-abiding citizens and those who were not so particular or honest.

By the time construction of the trail was completed the fourth mountain was already known locally as "Robber's Roost." A gang of thugs set up a permanent camp on the side of the mountain and were so secure there that they built a log cabin to serve as their permanent headquarters. These bandits were virtually assured of their security because of a decision they reached early on; they never bothered the Overland Company's stagecoaches or freight wagons so long as Jack Slade was around.

Some years later, however, (after Jack moved away from Virginia Dale) the robbers became far more bold. They robbed

Overland stages and freight trains with impunity, once taking a $60,000 cash payroll from a stage. That was too much for even the most tolerant of local residents, and they asked for help from the U.S. Army. A large group of soldiers left Fort (then "Camp") Collins and chased the bandits, who fled back into the mountains. It is said they buried the money somewhere in the vicinity of Robber's Roost—but the money has never been found.[4]

Some modern writers have suggested that Slade himself was somehow connected to the gang at Robbers' Roost and that he planned or led them in their robberies of the Overland stagecoaches. History does not support that revisionist theory. In addition to the fact that the robberies of the Overland stages occurred only after Slade had permanently left the area and was known to be living hundreds of miles away, armed robbery—and particularly robbery of the Overland Company, which Slade seemed to love—was completely out of character. Slade was cruel and he was a killer—but he was never known to be a thief. In his day, a thief (especially a horse thief) was the lowest form of humanity, and even the cold-blooded gunman probably never stooped that low.

It is a matter of record that during the time Jack Slade reigned at Virginia Dale, there were no robberies and no horse stealing from the Overland line in the area. There was never a theft from the Virginia Dale station. Outlaws like L.H. Musgrove and the others working the area knew enough to leave things alone at Slade's home base.

But the absence of robberies and thefts did not mean that everything on the Overland was peaceful and serene. To begin with, mere travel along the Trail West was an adventure—even without robberies. The trail passed through gloriously beautiful and rugged country with spectacular views of mountain peaks, buffalo herds, deer, antelope, and occasional mountain lions and bears. Eastern visitors were alternately frightened and awed by the beauty—and by the groups of Indian warriors who frequently sat on horseback, lined up atop one of the hogback

"Robbers' Roost," near Virginia Dale, was used as a safe haven for killers, robbers and rustlers until Jack Slade drove them away. (Courtesy Western History Collection, Denver Public Library)

ridges that followed the trail. The braves watched stoically as a stagecoach rumbled past.

But the stagecoach ride became particularly unpredictable and exciting if it happened to involve Slade himself as driver or companion. (Slade often took a turn at driving a coach from Fort Collins to Fort Halleck or vice versa, and even more often climbed aboard the stage to go into one of the communities on company business.)

On one of these trips a traveler from the eastern U.S.—a man clearly not accustomed to the wild ways of the frontier— became displeased with travel accommodations on the new stretch of trail. Regarding his trip northward from LaPorte toward Virginia Dale, this traveler wrote:

> Six wild mustangs were brought out and hitched to the stage, requiring a hostler[5] to each until the driver gathered up his line. When they were thrown loose the coach dashed off like a limited whirlwind, the wild, drunken jehu[6], in mad delight, keeping up the constant crack, crack with his snake

whip. The stage traveled for a time on the two off wheels, then lurched over and traveled on the other two by way of variety. Slade and his gang whooped and yelled like demons. Fortunately the passengers had taken the precaution before starting to secure an outside seat. The only way in which he was enabled to prevent the complete wreck of stage, necks, and everything valuable was finally by an earnest threat that he would report the whole affair to the company.[7]

In fact, the unhappy eastern writer seemed to have gotten off relatively easy compared to many other passengers. An increasing number of stagecoach trips now involved not just Jack Slade—but a thoroughly drunken Jack Slade, serving either as driver or guard. It seems likely that boredom brought on by a lack of trouble had caused Jack to fall deeply into the bottle. And as always, when he was drinking, Jack was mean.

On one trip south-bound out of LaPorte, Slade had been drinking heavily. He was not in the best of spirits while waiting impatiently at the station for the trip to get underway. Several times during the lengthy wait Slade had words with one of the male passengers who was complaining about some real or imagined inadequacy. After the stagecoach finally got under-way, Slade—who was riding shotgun for this trip—began brooding over the passenger's complaints. The longer he thought about it, the angrier Slade got. (It seems likely that he may have continued drinking as the trip progressed.)

At last unable to contain himself any longer, Slade drew his pistol and began shooting down through the roof of the coach. Slade either forgot—or didn't care—that the complaining passenger was just one of four customers aboard the stagecoach. As he shot into the car, Slade swore loudly at the man who had so irritated him.

The four startled passengers understandably panicked as Slade's bullets smashed through the stagecoach ceiling. Although the stage was moving rapidly down the rugged mountain trail, the passengers knew they couldn't stay where they were. One of them threw open the door and leaped out onto the prairie, followed immediately by the others. All were bruised and bloody but probably happy and unquestionably fortunate to have escaped with their lives.[8]

Once again, Slade avoided consequence from either the local law enforcement authorities or his own employers. Although it later became apparent that a number of customers wrote angry letters of complaint to Ben Ficklin, no action was taken against Slade. Buoyed by this immense freedom to do virtually anything he chose, Slade's behavior deteriorated further.

On another occasion when Slade had been drinking heavily he was either driving or riding shotgun on another of the coaches (history is unclear which role he was playing). When the coach pulled up at the Little Thompson relay station south of the present-day city of Loveland, Colorado, Slade was in a dark mood.

Stepping down from the stage Slade grabbed and pistol-whipped a man standing nearby, a man Slade thought was an Overland employee. Slade was furious because the man failed to recognize him and treat him properly upon his arrival. When he later learned that the man was simply a passenger and not an employee, Slade seemed to sober up. He went to the bloodied victim and apologized profusely, offering the man a drink as compensation. (History does not record whether the victim accepted.)

Then, whirling around to face the real employees, Slade pulled his pistol. As the men stepped back in terror, Slade shot a dog that was sleeping under a parked wagon. Then he kicked a pot of coffee into a small campfire, and finally challenged the two startled wranglers sitting there to fight him if they didn't like what he did. Neither man accepted the challenge.[9]

Now that Slade was spending more and more time with the bottle, his troubles were sky-rocketing. Unpleasant "incidents" involving him and his liquor occurred with increasing regularity on the trail. Yet while Slade himself spent considerable time

This illustration from Mark Twain's Roughing It *shows Slade and a hapless barkeeper. This illustration was titled "An Unpleasant View" and Twain writes the next instant, [the barkeeper] was one of the deadest men that ever lived."*

under the influence of alcohol, causing trouble, insulting passengers, shooting up equipment and generally terrorizing the territory, he tolerated no such behavior from his employees.

In summer 1862, one of Slade's drivers apparently forgot the rules. The driver became drunk while driving a stage between LaPorte and Livermore, Colorado. The intoxicated driver soon lost control of the horses. The animals bolted and eventually turned the stagecoach onto its side.

Slade was furious at the drunk driver, but, surprisingly, he was even more angry at whoever sold liquor to the teamster. Slade believed that only someone who was thoughtless and selfish would sell alcohol to a working stagecoach driver—a man who was responsible for the welfare of passengers and company equipment.

After giving the matter some consideration, Slade concluded that an establishment in LaPorte, Colorado, was most likely the source of the alcohol. He sent a messenger to order the owner of the store to never again sell alcohol to any of his drivers.

The indignant store owner, a man named George R. Sanderson, responded that he would darn well sell liquor to anyone he pleased! Given Slade's known reputation, it was not a wise response.

Four days after Slade was told to mind his own business, an Overland stagecoach stopped in front of the same LaPorte supply store. Slade and three of his employees climbed down from the stage and walked inside the store. Barely speaking, they took store owner Sanderson prisoner, led him outside and tied him to a hitching post where he could watch what was going on. Then the four men went back inside the store and began shooting.

They blasted bottles of expensive booze from the shelves. Rotgut whiskey, cheap wine and imported scotch shattered and smashed to the floor. The gunmen shot mirrors, windows, lamps, glassware, and everything else breakable. They shot gaping holes in the shelves and storage cabinets, the walls, ceiling, and floor. When the floor was sufficiently littered with broken glass and was awash with liquor, one of the men opened spigots on several barrels of molasses. Finally, Slade and his companions found a dozen bags of flour in an adjacent storeroom. They sliced open the bags and dumped the flour into the middle of the gummy, alcoholic, glass-littered gumbo on the floor.

At last satisfied with his work, Slade backed out of the store and stood surveying the damage. Apparently pleased with his handiwork, he stood with his back to the struggling shop keeper, reloaded his pistol, and dropped it back into his holster. Then at last he turned and walked over to George Sanderson.

"When I issue an order, sir," said Slade with mock politeness, "I expect you to obey without question!"

Slade and his men then climbed back aboard the stagecoach and vanished up the trail, leaving their victim still tied to the post.

Somewhat later—after he sobered up—Slade apparently realized that the LaPorte incident could become a major public relations embarrassment to him and his company. A few days later another Slade messenger arrived at the same bullet-riddled store. This messenger handed the surprised George Sanderson eight hundred dollars in cash and a note from Jack Slade. In the note Slade apologized for inflicting the damage and said he hoped there were no hard feelings.[10]

Although his remorse probably surprised Sanderson, the fact is that Slade almost always felt remorse about his drunken antics when he was sober. The problem was that he was sober with increasing infrequency.

Just a few weeks after the LaPorte incident—on October 15, 1862—Slade beat up a man in a barroom brawl at LaPorte. Although Slade lingered at the bar for another drink after the fight, no one apparently tried to detain him or arrest him.

Several days later Slade got into yet another brawl in a bar on Denver's Larimer street. This time he was not ignored. Two deputy U.S. marshals arrested Slade inside the bar and dragged him down to the city's new jail. After putting Slade in the cell the arresting officers learned that a warrant had been issued for Jack as a result of the earlier LaPorte brawl.

Court records indicate Slade appeared before the local magistrate, politely accepted his convictions on both counts, and quietly paid a fine for each of the fights. After leaving the court, Slade returned to the same Denver bar, apologized to the bartender for causing trouble, had two more drinks, and then quietly left for Virginia Dale.

But Slade's occasional public remorse over his alcoholic behavior was always short-lived; it vanished as soon as he began drinking the next time. Several weeks later, Slade was very nearly killed while on one of his drunken rampages.

On this occasion Slade walked into Mariano Medina's store and saloon, located on the Big Thompson River at the edge of the Colorado foothills near present-day Loveland.

Antonio Medina, the fourteen-year-old son of the owner, was alone in the store when Slade entered.

Slade was already visibly drunk and soon became abusive. He swore at the boy and gave him a shove when the teenager didn't move fast enough to suit. The boy—who was possibly too young to realize the danger involved or was afflicted with the common teenage fantasy of indestructibility—grabbed a rifle from behind the counter, cocked it, and pointed it at Slade's face. The startled Slade froze, possibly just sober enough to realize he must not shoot this boy.

Just as Antonio pulled the trigger, the boy's mother stepped into the room. Immediately recognizing what was happening, she slapped the barrel upward at the last critical moment, sending the bullet crashing harmlessly into the ceiling.

Slade stood unmoving and a tense silence descended on the room. The boy and his mother later said they expected Slade to pull his revolver and kill them both. Instead, Slade looked at the woman and her son, then turned and walked from the store without saying another word.[11]

As usual, the lesson was not long lasting. Only weeks after narrowly escaping with his life, Slade burst into the same Big Thompson relay station, and ordered the startled stationmaster there to fix him a cocktail. (History does not record whether this was the father of the boy who had nearly shot Jack in the first incident.) When the stationmaster was slow in responding to Slade's demand, Slade grabbed a double-barreled shotgun from its nearby resting place. Cocking both barrels he pointed the weapon at his employee's generous midsection.

"You'd better get movin'," said Slade.

The nervous stationmaster knocked down a couple of bottles and several glasses in his belated haste to comply with the order. At last, he successfully mixed a drink and carried it toward Slade.

"Put it on the barrels," ordered Slade, gesturing toward the weapon he still trained on the frightened man.

The stationmaster didn't know what to do and stood shaking.

"I said put it on the barrels," Slade repeated, indicating that the man was to balance the drink on the barrels of the shotgun, which Slade extended unmoving in the direction of the hapless stationmaster.

By now the poor man was shaking so hard he could barely comply. Gritting his teeth, he carefully balanced the drink glass on the shotgun, frightened half out of his wits that the drink would fall. At last, he backed away and—fortunately—the drink stayed perched on the barrels.

Laughing at both the man and the situation, Slade carefully retrieved the drink and swallowed it in a single gulp. Then he laid down the shotgun, slapped the stationmaster on the back and strode out of the building, laughing loudly.[12]

By this time everyone in Colorado and Wyoming knew about Jack Slade. If you found him sober, he was almost always a gentleman, a hard worker, a loyal husband, and a good friend. If you found him drunk, you might as well start praying; at these times he was a cold-blooded killer, a cruel employer, and a bully. And he was now drunk most of the time.

In spite of his well-earned reputation as a mean gunman, however, there was always that other side to Jack Slade. Although he apparently went to great lengths to keep his softer side well hidden from most people, the notorious killer could also be kind, considerate, and thoughtful when sober. He especially seemed to like small children, and sometimes went far out of his way to be kind or helpful to them. When sober, he was also always kind to animals and a perfect gentlemen to older ladies.

While he never referred to any incidence of kindness himself, a number of people claim that on one occasion a posse led by Slade shot and killed an outlaw who was the father of a young boy. The child, Jimmie Savoie, was slightly injured when the posse burned down the bandit's home before killing him. (There is a disagreement whether the cabin was in Colorado or Wyoming.)

Slade stood watching the cabin burn. When he heard the child screaming for help, Slade, witnesses said, personally rescued the boy from the burning building. The youth was coughing and apparently on the verge of passing out from smoke inhalation; these witnesses claim that Slade gave the child first aid.

After rescuing the boy and taking him back to civilization, Slade virtually adopted the child. There is evidence he paid to send the child and his widowed mother to Denver and saw to it they found a place to live. Thereafter, Slade sent money on regular occasions to make certain the child lived comfortably.[13]

(Jimmie Savoie grew up in Denver, supported by the Slades until he was sixteen years old. Jimmie then moved to Fort Bridger, Wyoming, and worked as a rancher. Later, he moved to Brown's Hole, Colorado, a favorite hideout of Butch Cassidy, and there owned a small ranch.)

Even if the story is true—as it apparently is—such seconds of kindness hardly compensated for the hours and days and months of meanness. Jack Slade knew he had to be tough to survive in his job, but he seemed to go overboard in enhancing his reputation as a heartless killer.

Slade was most often found these days squarely in the middle of one or another confrontation. The showdowns frequently ended in death for whoever had raised Slade's ire.

Slade's final public outburst as a resident of Colorado and supervisor for the Overland stagecoach line took place on the northern leg of the Overland Trail in Wyoming. The incident with the Overland Company became Slade's "final straw."

Slade had gone to Fort Halleck, a small army outpost located at the base of Elk Mountain. He was there on company business, but to no one's surprise, wound up spending an evening alone and drinking in a combination bar and sutler's store.[14] As usual, alcohol made him loud and abusive.

Soon, Slade was embroiled in an argument with a local cowboy. One of the men—no one seems to know which—

challenged the other to a fight. As frightened onlookers dived for cover, Slade and the cowboy both went for the weapons. As usual, Slade was quicker. He shot the cowboy in the chest.

Usually a shooting seemed to sober up Slade—or at least to calm him down—but shooting the cowboy seemed only to make Slade angrier. Whirling around, he next turned his attention to the bar itself, as if punishing the inanimate objects was somehow important to establishing his superiority. Slade took deliberate aim and began shooting bottles from the shelves one at a time. Next, he shot out all the windows and mirrors. Each time the pistol was empty, Slade calmly reloaded, and then resumed shooting everything that caught his attention in the bar.

Unbeknownst to Slade, however, someone had managed to slip out of the saloon and go for help. Three lawmen arrived at the bar while Slade was still blasting away. Fortunately for them, they arrived precisely at the moment when Slade had once again emptied his revolver. As Slade went through the motions of reloading the weapon, the lawmen burst through the swinging doors and ordered Slade to surrender.

Slade appeared bemused. He looked at the lawmen and—pointing his weapon at the ground—pulled the trigger to show that the revolver was empty. Then, smiling, Slade dropped the weapon back into his holster and raised his hands.

Since the wounded cowboy did not die, Slade was officially arrested on charges of attempted murder and drunk-and-disorderly conduct. Slade was put into the guardhouse briefly, but was released after promising he would never return to Fort Halleck.

The citizens, however, were fed up. Times were changing, and people had begun demanding law and order. Those responsible for law enforcement were not satisfied that Slade was necessarily a man of his word, and they were tired of Slade's antics up and down the front range in Colorado and Wyoming. A lawman wrote an angry letter to Ben Ficklin, Slade's boss, demanding that Slade not just avoid Fort Halleck, but that he be kept out of Wyoming. Forever! The letter would have far-reaching consequences.

Notes on Chapter Nine

1. Unpublished Manuscript 334 (Denver Public Library Western History Department), 1.

2. Museum notes (Fort Collins, CO: Historical Society, 1989).

3. *Ibid.*

4. Fort Collins Museum notes (1988).

5. A hostler is a man trained to handle horses, especially wild or untamed animals.

6. Stagecoach drivers were often called "jehu", apparently a reference to Jehu, the King of Israel, noted for his furious chariot attacks; see II Kings 9:11–36.

7. Evadene Burris Swanson, *Fort Collins Yesterdays* (Fort Collins, CO: Don-Art Printers, Inc., 1975), 89.

8. *Encyclopedia of Frontier Biography*, 1318.

9. *Ibid.*, 1319.

10. *A History of Larimer County*, 1114.

11. Some historians say Slade apologized before leaving the building, but neither the woman nor her son reported such an apology.

12. A *History of Larimer County*, 1114.

13. This story, found in numerous accounts, contains some of the same elements as the John Sarah family story (*Footprints on the Frontier*, 265). It seems likely that several incidents have been intermingled.

14. A sutler was a civilian who contracted to sell certain goods to the army. Sutlers frequently opened general retail stores near army posts.

SLADE THE HERO

FRONTIER AMERICA was changing rapidly. Although—except for one bitter little campaign in New Mexico, the Civil War was being fought far from Slade's country—the impact was real and severe. Many men went off to fight the war, and substantial numbers of them didn't come home again. Of greater overall significance was that the War was preoccupying the United States Army—meaning officers could not serve as Western law-enforcement authorities, and soldiers could not protect the West from increasingly frequent attacks by hostile Indians. With Confederates actively arming and agitating the Cheyenne, Lakota, Arapaho, and others against frontier settlers, law-abiding citizens were under attack.[1]

One result of all of this bloodletting was that local citizens tended to grow less and less tolerant of lawlessness and drunken revelry—even in the name of keeping the peace or defeating thieves. Towns were springing up all along the Overland and Oregon Trails. Increasingly, the people living in these communities demanded strict law and order. They insisted that all citizens obey the law and began hiring their own trustworthy law enforcement officers to make it happen. More than that, they demanded that gunslingers and killers leave the area and not come back.

Jack Slade often appeared to live in his own world, oblivious to what was going on around him. He appeared now not to notice the changes that were taking place in terms of law enforcement and attitudes about hired guns. He may not even have been aware that his continuing drunken tantrums were generating a shower of angry complaints from growing numbers of local citizens and alarmed officials. Many of those complaints went to the Overland Company offices in Saint Louis. Over time the flood of angry mail became more than even a tolerant Ben Ficklin could handle. Ficklin grew weary of dealing with mounting numbers of irate citizens and with damage claims filed against his company.

In the spring of 1862 Ficklin received a letter from the U.S. Marshal's office in Denver. The marshal warned that officers of the Overland Stage Company would be held personally responsible for any more damage inflicted by a drunken Slade. He also said that if Slade shot anyone else, the marshal would file criminal charges against Ben Ficklin and "others in a position of responsibility" within the company management.

At about the same time, another letter came from a LaPorte, Colorado, rancher. He said that all the citizens of the area were "fed up" with Slade and his staff, whom the letter-writer characterized in most uncomplimentary terms; "They are a drunken, carousing set in the main, and absolutely careless of the rights or feelings of the settlers."[2]

Ben Ficklin reluctantly and possibly somewhat belatedly came to the conclusion that Jack Slade had outlived his usefulness to the Overland Stage Company. The problem with such a decision was that it meant that Jack Slade had to be fired. The thought of facing Slade and telling him he was dismissed must have sent chills up and down Ficklin's back. For days he wrestled with the problem of how to fire a man of Slade's quick and often murderous temper.

After wrestling with the problem for several weeks Ficklin finally devised a plan. To implement the plan he first traveled to Denver. After checking around the town, he hired a veteran stage and freight administrator named Robert J. Spotswood to replace Slade as manager of the Overland Trail West. After the two men agreed that Spotswood would take the job, Ficklin dropped the bomb; he informed Spotswood that a part of his new job was that he was expected to personally dismiss Slade. (This may not have been because Ficklin feared Slade—it seems to have just been the way things were done at the time.)

The news shocked Spotswood, and for a while it looked like he might change his mind and not accept the job. He talked it over with his wife, who told him she would rather have an unemployed husband who was alive than an employed one who was dead. Spotswood's friends were no more encouraging; they were convinced that when he told Slade what was going on, Slade would immediately kill him. All of them— wife, children, friends—begged Spotswood not to accept the job. Spotswood wanted the job badly, though, and finally accepted Ficklin's offer in spite of the risk involved.

Spotswood's friends couldn't believe his foolishness. They were distraught with what they considered a foolhardy decision. So certain were they that Spotswood would be murdered by Slade that these friends threw the new Overland Trail boss a farewell party. In a somber affair, guest after guest downed his drink without smiling, walked over to Spotswood, and solemnly shook his hand good-bye. Most of the guests were convinced they would never see Spotswood again. Several wiped tears from their cheeks as they bade Spotswood one last farewell.

The following day Spotswood caught the northbound stagecoach to LaPorte, where he spent another night probably agonizing about the task that faced him. Early the next morning he continued northward to Virginia Dale. One can only imagine his thoughts during that long, bumpy ride, and— even worse—upon finally arriving at Jack Slade's home. Spotswood stepped down from the stage, straightened his vest, and walked determinedly toward the building.

Jack Slade was sitting on the front porch, leaning a chair back against the wall. He watched with curiosity as this lone passenger left the stage and walked toward him. Slade didn't speak, even when the stranger walked directly up to the chair. Without preamble, Spotswood broke the news that he was the new manager of the Overland West division and that Slade was fired. Then Spotswood took a step backward, clenched his jaw, and waited.

Spotswood later told friends that the expression on Slade's face never changed. Slade stared at Spotswood for several agonizingly long seconds. At last he dropped the front of the chair back onto the floor and slowly stood up. Talking more to himself than to Spotswood, Slade mumbled, "I've been expecting this."

He motioned Spotswood to follow him inside the building. Then, to the total surprise of Spotswood, it was the Dr. Jekyll Slade with whom he worked for the next several hours. Slade calmly went about the process of initiating an orderly transition from his supervision to that of Spotswood. The new supervisor would later comment that he had never met anyone who was more polite or more thorough in making certain a replacement had everything he needed to carry out the assignment.

The men worked together all day, going over records, discussing on-going projects, talking about employees, even brainstorming ideas to improve the line. They ate dinner together, and to all appearances it was an entirely friendly social gathering. When Spotswood was finally taken to his room for the night, Jack began packing.

By early the following morning, Jack and Virginia Slade had stored excess personal belongings in a shed and had loaded the necessities into a couple of suitcases and one large wooden crate. Slade asked Spotswood to hold everything for him until he sent for it after relocating. The most feared gunman in the West then shook Spotswood's hand warmly and wished him luck in the new assignment. The Slades then climbed aboard their waiting horses and headed north along the Overland Trail.

One western writer claims that Jack was actually happy to be leaving Colorado because a warrant had been issued for his arrest in Julesburg, charging him with murder (presumably that of Jules Beni).³ This information is not repeated in other accounts of that era and probably is not true. In actual fact, Slade had been unofficially exonerated—by the Code of the West—in every killing attributed to him since joining the Russell, Majors and Waddell freight line.

Although Slade's activities in the months immediately following his dismissal are not clearly accounted for, some reports indicate Slade moved first to Fort Bridger in the far southwestern corner of what became Wyoming. According to this information, Slade opened his own small freight company there, hauling goods between Fort Bridger, Salt Lake City, and Denver. While the line apparently did reasonably well, Slade sold it a short time later.⁴ No record exists of any run-ins between Slade and locals at Fort Bridger during this time period—but that should not be overly surprising. As always, when Slade was very busy handling a major assignment, he worked efficiently and diligently to get the job done.

Several years prior to this time, Slade had made one trip to Montana as a driver for the old freight line company. During that journey he had fallen in love with the wide-open spaces there and believed the future was still bright in Montana. It was an area mostly unsettled by white men. It seemed possible that no one there had even heard of Slade, that by going to Montana he actually would have a chance to start over. Slade is said to have confided to close friends that he had always dreamed of becoming a respectable rancher or a businessman, apparently believing he was fully in control of both his temper and his drinking. Virginia also seemed excited about the prospect of a new lifestyle. She encouraged Jack to sell his little freight company and move north. Some years later Virginia commented that the trip northward to Montana was "perhaps the happiest time of my life."

The Slades headed for Virginia City, the only place in Montana Jack had ever been. It was a lovely, bustling community

This photo is identified in the Denver Public Library collection only as Slade's Ravenswood ranch; the individuals are not named. However, when the photo is enlarged (at right), the man on the left and the woman show a striking resemblance to Jack and Virginia Slade. (Courtesy Denver Public Library)

surrounded by rich rangeland. This was exactly what Jack and Virginia envisioned, and Virginia apparently was entirely taken with the beauty of the area.

Within a few weeks the Slades had purchased two small ranches just outside Virginia City. The first—a 160-acre tract was located on Trail Creek, about eight miles east of Virginia City. It was here that the Slades would live. Jack already knew the construction business—he had built or supervised the building of dozens of relay stations all along the Oregon and Overland Trails. Excited by his new life and his new ranch, Slade worked hard and soon had built a house for his wife, modern and efficient by the standards of the time. They named the ranch Spring Dale.

A little farther north Slade bought another 360 acres of land on the Madison River. On this ranch he began raising

These two people are unidentified in the photo at left, however they resemble other images thought to be Jack and Virginia Slade. See drawing of Slade (p. 32) and photograph of Virginia (p. 63). (Courtesy Denver Public Library)

dairy cattle, and soon was in the business of selling milk and cheese to Virginia City stores.[5] The Slades called this place Ravenswood.

Slade also turned to the profession he knew best (other than gunslinging). He purchased several wagons and a dozen horses and opened a short-haul freight business operating throughout southeastern Montana. The freight company, like the ranches, apparently prospered from the beginning. Within a short time, Jack had acquired more than two dozen wagons and several hundred horses, and had built several relay stations. Business was booming, and the Slades prospered.

For a brief time everything seemed to go well for the Slades. They seemed to be well-liked and fully accepted in the community. The Slades blossomed as civic leaders, and Jack's opinion was sought out in various matters of general concern.

Jack had wanted to start life anew, had dreamed of becoming just an ordinary citizen, and now it was happening. He had wanted to shed his old image as gunfighter, and that, too, was happening. Jack was actually respected.

He blossomed under this set of circumstances and fit in well as a pioneer rancher. In fact, Slade was soon a legitimate hero to the community of Virginia City.

By the time the Slades moved there, Virginia City and the adjacent Nevada City boasted a population of five thousand permanent residents, plus several hundred itinerant miners, drifters and travelers at any given moment. Unfortunately, the towns were extremely isolated. The two communities together were generally known simply as Alder Gulch, Montana, a bustling mining center that relied entirely on the outside world for day-to-day necessities. Food and all other vital supplies for Virginia City and other nearby mining settlements had to be shipped to the community from Saint Louis. To reach its destination, everything had to make a laborious journey up the Missouri River by boat to Fort Benton, Montana. There it was loaded onto freight wagons and hauled more than two hundred miles farther—over rugged roads and through dangerous territory—to reach the mining communities. It was a perilous life line.

In 1863 the entire Frontier West was gripped by a severe drought. Crops and grassland withered, cattle and wildlife died, and people from Albuquerque to Virginia City became desperate for food. Many Cheyenne, Arapaho, and Kiowa Indians—especially those who were counting on the new white settlers to supply them with necessities—starved to death. The problem was all the worse because the Great Plains Indian War was nearing its peak; 1863 was the second bloodiest year of that protracted, decades-long confrontation between Native Americans and white intruders. Freight wagons and freight boats were under constant attack, and many of them couldn't get through to the starving people. Settlers soon found it impossible to get anything that had to be shipped to the West from somewhere else.

Because of the dangerous "Indian situation" and the severe drought, the vital supply ship headed for Virginia City in the summer of 1863 could travel upstream only as far as the mouth of the Milk River. That left the badly needed food and other supplies nearly seven hundred miles from Virginia City, and a good five hundred miles from the nearest army post that offered any protection from the Indian raiders who dominated the territory. The land that lay between the Milk River and Fort Benton was ruled by Blackfeet Indians who hated whites and were starved for food. Virtually no knowledgeable frontiersman knowingly crossed Blackfeet territory, and the few who stumbled into the region by accident were never seen again. Virginia City appeared doomed to starvation.

The Slades were not in any immediate personal danger. The Madison River was low, but it did still contain water, and Slade's dairy farm continued to do well. That meant the Slades had meat and dairy products, and most likely at least some crops in a home garden. However, the rest of the community was not so fortunate. Apart from the critical shortage of some food items, they had no way to get many of the needed commodities essential to daily life — things like spare parts for mining equipment, guns and ammunition for hunting or self preservation, certain non-perishables, and many other items.

Desperation soon set in. The citizens of Alder Gulch needed someone brave enough — or foolhardy enough — to organize and direct a wagon train across the seven hundred miles of Indian territory, retrieve the needed supplies, re-cross the Indian land, and return safely to Virginia City. Who better for the job than gentleman rancher and community leader Jack Slade?

When the scope of the problem became clear, citizen Slade actually volunteered for the assignment. He immediately set about organizing the manpower needed, and based on his long experience along the frontier, even laid out roads, built bridges, obtained necessary supplies of animals and hay, and otherwise put together an emergency party. The citizens were elated;

obviously no one was better qualified than Jack Slade to undertake such a dangerous assignment.

Once it was decided that this veteran frontiersman would head the rescue project, all of Slade's experience and natural skills blossomed. This was his kind of project; he alone was in command and he alone was responsible for all the decisions. He rose to the challenge.

Possibly because everyone knew what would happen if the project failed, Slade had little trouble finding volunteers to make the trip with him—and to make ready for it. Within days he had two dozen men busy constructing the necessary supply wagons, and two dozen more working on gathering horses and other items needed for the trip. Simultaneously, Slade recruited and trained about twenty other volunteers who would actually make the trip. He spent several days selecting these men, chosen for their ability to defend themselves with guns, survive the rigors of a long trip through hostile territory, and most importantly—their willingness to take orders from Jack Slade.

But manpower and wagons were not the only problem for this rescue effort. This trip was not across an established wagon road. Miles of road had to be laid out, bridges had to be built across gullies and streams. The scope of the undertaking would have frightened off most men—but none of it was too tough for Jack Slade. Literally within a few weeks, he had everything ready for the dangerous trip.

The citizens of Virginia City held a huge send-off party for the men who would make the trek. It was a strange party. The planned trip held out great hopes. Thousands of citizens depended on the success of these intrepid adventurers—yet virtually everyone was aware of the enormous danger that faced the men undertaking this gallant task. Citizens did their best to put on happy faces, but everyone knew the truth; there was little probability that those who set out on the trip would ever come back again.

Unfortunately, there is no first-hand account of the trip. It is known with certainty that in an arduous five-month journey, Jack Slade and his companions reached the river boat, off-loaded the supplies, and then returned safely to Virginia City. Not a man was lost on the trip nor were any supplies. There are suggestions that the rescue party fought several prolonged battles with Blackfeet Indians. All that is known for certain is that eventually Jack Slade and all of his volunteers returned triumphantly to Alder Gulch, bringing with them a wagon train of supplies vital to survival for several thousand persons. It was a truly amazing accomplishment and one that could have been achieved by very few men. As one writer put it:

> Slade organized a train, went and got the supplies, fought off Indians, built his own roads, and in the dead of a Montana winter, which is something in itself, brought them in safely without loss of a man or an item of goods![6]

There has always been speculation and great curiosity about the journey. Did the men, as suggested above, fight off repeated Indian attacks? What perils did they overcome in the long trip? Who were the heroes? How did they survive in the wilderness, and against all odds?

The only thing known with absolute certainty is that Slade and his companions completed the journey in five months and two days and returned safely to Virginia City on December 10, 1863. And the most amazing fact was not that they returned home with all the supplies, it is that Slade also brought back every single man who accompanied him on the journey.

Jack Slade was now a genuine hero to the Montanans. At this point in his life he could have been elected mayor, on to some other high office, had he chosen to become a politician. For the first time in his life, Jack was a genuine, unquestioned champion of the people, adored by women, respected by men, loved by children.

It was, of course, too good to last.

NOTES ON CHAPTER TEN

1. For a complete discussion of the Confederate "Indian strategy" and its impact on the frontier, see Scott, *Blood at Sand Creek*, (Caldwell, ID: Caxton Printers, 1994).

2. *Fort Collins Yesterdays*, 90.

3. *Bloodletters and Badmen*, 343.

4. *History of Larimer County*, 1319.

5. *The Hanging of Bad Jack Slade*, 35.

6. Unpublished Manuscript 334, 4.

CHAPTER ELEVEN

SLADE THE Villain

MAYBE THINGS WERE simply too quiet for Jack Slade. Maybe, in spite of his life-long ambition to be a respectable businessman and rancher, his real personality couldn't handle serenity or respect. Maybe at heart he was simply an evil man. Shortly after returning from the epic journey that saved Virginia City, it all came crashing down again.

Jack rode into Virginia City one morning to purchase a load of lumber with which to build a new cabin on the ranch where he pastured his dairy cows, Ravenswood. At the local sawmill his famous temper and the "Mr. Hyde" personality erupted.

This was an era when men bargained for everything; there were no "suggested retail prices." Most items exchanged hands as the result of trades, and it was simply expected that prices were negotiable. Even as cities were established and merchants began posting "hard" prices for some wares, many men continued to bargain for everything they acquired. Jack Slade was such a man.

On this particular day Slade was trying to negotiate for a better price on his lumber. The lumber dealer was trying to switch over to the new "set price" way of doing business and was in no mood to haggle with Jack Slade. It wasn't long before the two men got into a heated argument.

The lumberman was prominent Virginia City businessman Nathaniel P. H. Langsford, the owner of the sawmill. He had a reputation as a hard worker with a short fuse, and he had little tolerance for those who disagreed with him.

According to some accounts of the confrontation that morning, Slade was less concerned about the price of the lumber than about his credit. He had expected to purchase the lumber on his signature, possibly reasoning that because of his hero status no one was going to turn him down. That turned out not to be the case with Nathaniel Langsford. Langsford flat told Jack that he did not know him—and he wasn't about to extend credit to a man he didn't know, hero or not. The fact is that Langsford probably had heard something about Slade and his credit. In spite of his current hero's reputation, Slade also was deeply in debt to most of the businessmen in town, and there was no indication he was about to pay any of his bills.

Slade couldn't believe there was anyone in the West who didn't know him—either as hero in Montana or as deadly gunfighter in Wyoming and Colorado. His ego probably also found it difficult to believe anyone would deny him credit. His anger and resentment boiled to the surface.

There are some indications that Slade struggled with what to do and how to handle this situation. He was, after all, committed to establishing a new identity and new reputation in Virginia City. To his credit, he avoided drawing his pistol and settling this argument as he had so many others in earlier days, even after the argument degenerated into a shouting match.

Instead of shooting, Slade began to reason with Langsford. Slade explained that without an extension of credit, he could not buy the lumber he needed and which had already been loaded onto Slade's flatbed wagon. It was only logical, therefore, that the lumberman extend him credit. In response, Langsford ordered several of his employees to unload the lumber.

Slade looked surprised but said nothing as the men set about their work. After fifteen minutes of hard work, the lumber had been unloaded and Slade's wagon once again stood empty. About the time they completed the task of unloading the lumber, though, Slade appeared to admit defeat. Witnesses—apparently meaning Langsford and his employees—say that Slade told Langsford that he was not going to argue any further and that he would pay cash for the lumber after all.

Sighing, Langsford ordered his men to load the lumber onto Slade's wagon a second time. The employees went to work again and in a half hour had once again lashed the lumber to Slade's flatbed wagon.

When the task was completed, Slade began counting out money—but he counted out an amount substantially less than the figure asked by the lumberman. Langsford was furious. He insisted on full payment at his asking price. Just as strongly, Slade insisted on purchasing the lumber at the lesser price.

Once again Langsford ordered his men to unload the wagon. Once again they complied, sweating and straining to off-load the lumber a second time as Jack Slade stood silently watching.

After the wagon had been unloaded for the second time, Slade again began a conversation with Langsford. After a brief time, both men seemed to calm down a great deal. Eventually they struck a new deal and shook on the agreement. Langsford called his employees back, and for the third time they loaded the lumber onto Slade's wagon.

But once again, when the wagon was completely loaded, Slade counted out the wrong amount of money.

This time, the furious Langsford went for his gun. It was a foolish error and could have cost him his life. Fortunately for Langsford, just at that critical moment several bystanders jumped between Langsford and Slade, one of them literally holding Jack's arm to keep him from drawing his revolver.

Onlookers were surprised at this intervention. Normally, when men went for their guns, everyone else dived for cover. Possibly because of Jack's new reputation as a hero, or because civilization was finally beginning to settle on this mining town, people had begun to think and act differently. Whatever the cause, the bystanders prevented bloodshed.

Then—presumably because Jack really was a town hero—one of the bystanders offered to pay any difference between the amount tendered by Slade and the amount that Langsford thought was fair. After a few minutes everyone present agreed to the settlement. Slade paid what he thought was fair, the bystander paid the difference, the lumberman was satisfied, and Slade finally departed with the lumber.

Slade was probably pleased with himself. He had purchased a wagon load of lumber for much less than the asking price, and he had done so without bloodshed. To a man like Slade, that was a remarkable accomplishment. He also most likely reasoned that the dispute was now a dead issue and the subject would never again be mentioned.[1]

Actually, however, the lumberyard dispute was the final straw for the law-abiding citizens of Virginia City, Montana, many of whom knew a great deal more about Jack Slade than Slade presumed. It turns out that the men who paid the difference at the lumberyard did so to save the life of their friend, Nathaniel Langsford, and not because of Jack's new-found hero status.

Most people in town did not personally know Slade. Even though most were grateful to him for the long journey he had made on their behalf, most also knew of his earlier reputation. Stories about Jack Slade had circulated throughout the West for half a decade. Men settling in Montana had migrated there from places like Wyoming and Colorado where Slade's reputation was badly tarnished. Some of these men also knew something else which caused great resentment; Jack Slade was interfering with their plans to establish a quiet, law-abiding community.

At about the time Jack and Virginia Slade began trying to build respectability for themselves, other settlers in Virginia City had already decided they would never again tolerate gunslingers or troublemakers. A dedicated group of local citizens swore an oath that they would pay with their lives, if necessary, to keep out undesirable men—killers and gamblers and thieves. Men like Jack Slade.

A number of local citizens had been warily watching Slade ever since he arrived in their community. And they had already decided that the first time Jack Slade stepped out of line, he had to be dealt with seriously.

In order to control or prevent crime in the sparsely populated area, the local cattlemen and businessmen earlier had formed a "vigilance committee"—the famous Montana "Committee of 100." The Committee was the first and perhaps best known of the vigilante groups that virtually took over law-enforcement responsibilities in a number of western locales in the second half of the nineteenth century.

In these vigilante groups, local citizens drew their strength from numbers and from unity of purpose. Sometimes when these civilians went about their law-enforcement duties, they wore hoods or masks to conceal their identities. They usually worked at night, and they operated with lightning speed. Normally mild-mannered store owners and bookkeepers took on new identities after dark. They donned masks and guns, and set about finding—and hanging—undesirables who had come to their town.

If an undesirable character showed up in Virginia City, the vigilantes decided almost without any discussion, how to deal with the issue. The answer was nearly always terminal for the newly-arrived bad guy. In the middle of some dark night several hooded men would grab the troublemaker. He was taken before another, larger group of hooded men who held a five or ten minute "trial" on the spot. During the trial, charges against the suspect were articulated and the arrested man was sometimes given an opportunity to speak. Immediately thereafter the committee pronounced sentence.

Often the sentence was for the undesirable person to leave town immediately—that night—or else. The "or else" meant hanging from the nearest tree. Very few of the men faced with that choice declined the invitation to move on. And on those occasions when the vigilantes decided that it was already too late for second chances, the punishment was hanging. In such instances the punishment was immediate. Citizens awakened the next morning to find the condemned man swinging from the nearest suitable tree or telegraph pole.

The Montana Committee of 100 had let it be known far and wide that the laws of Montana would be fully enforced and that the Territory would no longer tolerate crime or criminals. They had warned openly and repeatedly that they would deal harshly with troublemakers who ignored their threats. The warnings were published in newspapers, sometimes printed on posters that were nailed to trees, and were the subject of considerable talk. In addition, most had seen the results of the on-spot trials. Everyone in the West knew about the Committee of 100.

Ironically, there is compelling evidence that Jack Slade was, himself, one of the vigilantes for a short time. It appears that he actively participated in many of the early vigilante trials and hangings around Virginia City.

One of the leaders of the vigilantes was John Xavier Beidler, known to his friends as X. Beidler. Beidler had a reputation as a man who would tolerate no evil. As a pioneer in Kansas several years earlier, he was known for having organized local citizens to drive undesirables out of a number of communities. Now a resident of Virginia City, Beidler was determined to repeat his Kansas successes.

When he and a dozen other local citizens formed the Vigilance Committee, it was Beidler who wrote the famous oath:

> We the undersigned, uniting ourselves together for the laudable purpose of arresting thieves and murderers and recovering stolen property, do pledge ourselves on our sacred honor, each to all others, and solemnly swear that we will reveal no secrets, violate no laws of right, and never desert each other, or our stand or justice, so help us God.

Ironically, Beidler was also an outspoken admirer of Jack Slade, whom he knew to be a loyal, friendly, helpful neighbor even before he became a real-life hero to the citizens of Alder Gulch. Slade and Beidler became friends almost the moment Slade settled in Montana. As he had done in other settings, Slade apparently treated his neighbors with respect and was there to lend a helping hand when needed. He and Beidler shared many relaxed evenings around a campfire before the Slades built their ranch homes. Beidler also was fond of Virginia Slade, and in his own memoirs told of pleasant times socializing with the Slades:

> I met him at his ranch on the Madison River when he lived in a tent, and his wife cooked a good dinner for us. We communed on many occasions as friends. Slade was an honest man and did not like a thief—but was a very dangerous man when drinking.[2]

At a time when independent thinking, physical strength, and fortitude were highly respected, the influential Beidler was not the only one in Alder Gulch to think highly of Jack Slade—when he was sober. The town's newspaper publisher, who doubled as a private tutor and a voice coach, Thomas J. Dimsdale, spoke regularly of the impressive attributes of Jack Slade. According to his own admission, Dimsdale once toyed with the idea of asking Slade to consider seeking election to the town council.

Apparently, X. Beidler and a number of others thought enough of Jack Slade to invite him to join the newly-forming vigilantes. Although it was still relatively new, the Montana "vigilance group" was already extremely active when Jack moved to Virginia City. While the records of the vigilantes are forever sealed, a number of men with first-hand knowledge say that Slade readily accepted the invitation and joined the vigilantes.

Beidler strongly hints at such an affiliation in his own diary, published years later as "*X. Beidler: Vigilante*. So does journalist Dimsdale, both in his newspaper articles and in his subsequent book, *The Vigilantes of Montana*. Said Dimsdale of

Slade's vigilante affiliation: "He openly boasted of it, and said he knew all that they knew!"[3]

Months earlier—on February 21, 1863—a group of the masked vigilantes "arrested" a local gold miner named George Ives, whom they accused of murdering a fellow miner in a claim dispute. (There is little doubt of Ives' guilt; there were eyewitnesses to the slaying.) Ives was tried, convicted, and promptly hanged in front of his cabin, all in a period of about ten minutes.

The following night the vigilantes arrested another miner, one Nick Tiebat, whom they accused of participation in the same murder for which Ives had already been dispatched. Fighting for his life, Tiebat blurted out a confession that was shocking in its scope. He said that almost all of the rampant crimes in the area—including murders, bank robberies and cattle rustling—were being carried out by Virginia City Sheriff Henry Plummer and his gang of twenty deputies! The vigilantes, who already suspected that Plummer was a crook, thanked Tiebat for the information—and then hanged him anyway.

The next night, vigilantes went all over the Territory visiting the houses of Sheriff Plummer, his deputies, and anyone else suspected of involvement in criminal activity. At each home the vigilantes tacked onto the door a piece of paper bearing the inscription "3-7-77." The cryptic message was already recognized throughout the West as a warning that the vigilantes were about to strike. If a man receiving such a notice wanted to live he had better get out of town quickly!

Like most other bullies, however, Plummer thought he was just too tough for anyone else to handle. He and his men met the next morning, probably to discuss the warning notes, but took no obvious action in response. It was a fatal error.

Over the next six weeks, the Vigilance Committee systematically hunted down the sheriff and his deputies, hanging them one by one. Fifteen of these "lawmen" had already been hanged when the final six deputies were arrested simultaneously and

hauled into downtown Virginia City. Five of these men—
Boone Helm, Hayes Lyons, Clubfoot George, Frank Parish, and
Jack Gallagher—were hanged in broad daylight at the intersection of Van Buren and Wallace Streets, the busiest intersection
in town. A noisy crowd of gold miners, ranchers, and townsfolk
cheered the hangings.⁴ There is strong reason to believe that
Jack Slade was one of the hooded vigilantes who participated in
the mass execution.

By now the message was crystal clear to criminal and law-
abiding citizen alike: Alder Gulch was not going to tolerate
lawlessness. Any criminal who wanted to stay alive needed to
find work in some other part of the country.

Ironically, the law-and-order Committee of 100 was officially headed by a powerful young Alder Gulch rancher named
Jim Williams. Yes, this was the same Jim Williams who had
bested Slade in that famous confrontation with both pistols
and fists several years earlier, when both men were part of a
wagon train headed from Colorado to Montana.

Friends say that Williams shook his head sadly and sighed
deeply when he first learned that Jack Slade had moved to Virginia City. He warned others that there was no way to avoid
trouble with this man—that, sooner or later, Slade's terrible
temper would explode. The Committee, he said, needed to
keep a careful watch on Slade and be prepared to move quickly
when the time came. William's prophetic warning proved accurate in less than a year.

The first time Slade crossed the vigilantes was the incident
at the lumberyard. Word reached Jim Williams that Jack Slade
had confronted a local businessman and might have shot him
had not a crowd intervened. Williams called a hasty meeting of
others on the Vigilance Committee and briefed them on what
he personally knew of Slade's unsavory reputation.

The Committee agreed that something had to be done at
once. The problem was that in spite of his generally terrible reputation while drinking, Slade had, in fact, become something of a

respected local citizen. He had calmed down a great deal from his earlier days in Wyoming and Colorado—and he was, after all, a savior to the citizens of Virginia City and neighboring Nevada City. After a brief discussion, the vigilantes decided that Slade would be allowed to live—a mildly surprising compromise—but also that he would have to leave the Territory at once.

While historians don't agree on exactly what happened next, it is clear the Committee somehow sent word to Slade to get out of town. Some writers believe Williams personally delivered the warning, while others say the warning was sent by messenger. The latter version is more likely true. In fact, one of those 3-7-77 notes may have been tacked to Slade's cabin door.

As always, Jack Slade apparently was taken by surprise to find that someone didn't like him. Virginia Slade later told friends that Jack was "stunned" when was told he was not welcome in the area and that he must quickly leave Virginia City and never return. However, in much the same manner that he accepted his dismissal from the freight line back in Colorado, he seemed to calmly and rationally accept this latest setback.

At first, Slade did not appear to resist the order in any way. In fact, he told the vigilantes, presumably through their messenger, that he would leave both the town and the Montana Territory at once. He apparently went so far as to tell his wife to begin packing. He may even have suggested to Virginia that he leave immediately to find a new place for them to settle and that he would send for her later.

Whatever the truth, Slade actually did get ready to leave town. He quietly packed his saddlebags, slung a bedroll over his horse, and rode away from his ranch home.

Then two things went wrong at the same time. The first difficulty was that the trail "out of town" passed *through* the town; to get from Jack's house to anyplace else he had first to ride through Virginia City. It was like telling a child that he must go on a strict diet—as soon as he passed through the candy store one last time!

Secondly, Slade had a habit of brooding when things went wrong. And he usually brooded over a bottle of whiskey, usually at some local bar. And when he was drinking, Jack got real mean.

Things were going very wrong now for Jack Slade, and he began brooding. He brooded about being kicked out—first from Wyoming, then from Colorado, and now from Montana. And before he left the area, he began to drink as he thought about all his problems. Somewhere along the way he met up with six of his closest (and apparently most unsavory) friends. Among this group was Bill Fairweather, a gold miner.[5] Fairweather and the others soon joined Slade in a drinking spree.

Before long, Jack Slade was "in his cups." In that alcohol-clouded state of mind, Slade decided it would be a good idea to ride into Virginia City and let the town know that although he was leaving, he was not happy about it.

Slade and his companions reached town about eight that evening—precisely the moment that the curtain was going up on a traveling road show. Tickets for the performance cost $2.50 each, but nearly everyone in town—including children—were there for the performance. One of the actresses in the show, a dancer named Kate Harper, had just strolled onto stage dressed in a scanty ballet costume for the opening number. Suddenly, the door of the makeshift theater burst open and in staggered a drunken Jack Slade.

The appearance of Slade had an electrifying effect on both the crowd and the performers; time seemed to stand still and no one in the building breathed. No one except Jack Slade.

One of those in the crowd was vigilante X. Beidler. Writing his own memoirs later, Beidler says that "...in a loud and vulgar voice, (Slade) ordered her to take off the balance of her dress."[6] Beidler says that at this point everyone in the theater made a hasty evacuation—including all the actors. Jack Slade eventually also left the theater.

Slade staggered back to the hitching post and rejoined his six drunk companions. At this point, some believe Jack may have tried to go back to his ranch and to Virginia, possibly to sober up. Beidler and several other witnesses say that Slade actually rode out of town toward his home, but the trip was a disaster.

First, Slade rode his horse into the path of a milk wagon, causing it to run off the road and overturn in a ditch, spilling its cargo. Then Slade confronted two of his own ranch hands—Dan Harding and Charley Edwards—and after shouting at them for several minutes, apparently struck both of them several times. (Some accounts say that Slade "beat" the men, but there is no evidence either man was marked by the confrontation.)

By now, Slade apparently gave up any possible consideration he had entertained about going home to sleep off his drunk. He and his companions turned around and headed back into the heart of Virginia City. They brazenly rode up the main street of the city—and Jack rode his horse directly *inside* the first bar he came to.

Without dismounting, Slade ordered the bartender to fix him a drink. The startled bartender might not have done so, but Slade had his Colt revolver out of the holster and waved it menacingly as he spoke. As other patrons scrambled for cover, the bartender handed Jack his whiskey.

Then, as he drank, Slade began shooting. Not at people, this time; he was shooting at things. As had become his habit, glass things were his primary target—bottles, mirrors, windows, even light fixtures. Slade seemed to enjoy the sound of shattering glass.

Sitting calmly astride his horse, drink in his left hand and pistol in his right, Slade blasted everything in sight. No one knows for sure how many times Slade emptied his pistol, reloaded, and fired again, but it must have been many times. Dozens of bottles were broken, and nearly every other item of glass in sight was shattered.

Eventually, there was nothing else to break. Slade looked around the bar for several minutes, apparently searching for something else to shoot. Disappointed that everything was already broken, he finally rode leisurely back out into the street.

And rode his horse into the next bar he came to. According to newspaperman Thomas Dimsdale, this was Dorris's Saloon. Slade was ordered by the bartender to leave, and Dimsdale says Slade responded by drawing his revolver and "threatening to kill the gentleman who spoke to him." Then Slade purchased a bottle of wine and tried to get his horse to take a drink of the bottle. Wrote Dimsdale: "This was not considered an uncommon performance, as he often entered saloons and commenced firing at lamps, causing a wild stampede."[7]

Writing a series of articles for his newspaper the *Montana Post* some months later, Dimsdale suggested that local citizens in a rough-and-tumble mining town had become more or less used to Slade's drunken raids. Dimsdale said that "on several occasions" in the six months prior to this particular night, Slade and two or three of his friends had galloped their horses through town, firing their revolvers in the air. Such incidents commonly ended when Slade rode his horse into a bar or store, shot up the interior, and insulted the proprietor. Dimsdale noted that a day or so later, a contrite Slade always reappeared at the bar or store, apologized profusely, and paid for the damage inflicted.

But in this particular bar on this particular night, the crowd seemed unwilling to go along with Slade's rampage. As a crowd watched silently—many of them crouched behind overturned tables—the scene that had occurred moments earlier in a neighboring saloon was repeated. Once again Slade sat on his horse and drank, then shot up the interior of the bar while patrons dived for cover.

Slade's six drinking buddies accompanied him on each raid. They occasionally joined him in shooting up the bars—and the more they all drank, the more prolific they became.

There is some confusion about how long the shooting spree lasted. Some writers claim Slade and his companions were in town for a full week, shooting up various places of business and getting into all sorts of scrapes. Given the mood of the town and the efficiency of the Committee of 100, that version hardly seems possible; the spree probably lasted only a few hours. The only two eyewitnesses to have recorded the incident and later reported it in book form—vigilante X. Beidler and newspaperman Thomas Dimsdale—both say the rampage lasted fewer than eight hours.

Even in a short time, however, the destruction wrought by Slade and his friends was devastating. Beidler wrote that by dawn the following morning Virginia City's main business district:

> ...appeared as if it had been struck by a cyclone. Hitch rails were torn down. Gold scales, hurled through saloon windows, lay in twisted ruins on the glass-littered plank walks. Raw bullet holes splintered doors and shuttered windows.[8]

However long the rampage went on was just a little bit too long from the point of view of the Committee of 100. It was still dark on the evening of March 10, or the early-morning hours of March 11, 1864[9]. Jack Slade was going through his routine of shooting up the interior of yet another bar when suddenly a group of armed men entered the building from several directions.

Slade looked surprised at the brazenness of these men— entering a bar he was shooting up. A second look told him that all of these men were pointing their weapons at him simultaneously. Slade paused, pistol pointing toward the ceiling, and for a long moment simply stared. After a tense several seconds, Slade finally slid his revolver back into the holster and raised his hands, a smile playing at the corners of his mouth.

This was only the second time in his career that Slade had been taken prisoner. The veteran gunman looked from man to man, then gently (and unsteadily) slid down from his horse, and, again obligingly, raised his hands into the air. Slade knew he could not face so many men, and knew that they had come to enforce their order that he leave the Territory.

In an unusual turn of events, Virginia City's newly-appointed sheriff, J. M. Fox, showed up and took custody of the prisoner. Slade was formally arrested by Sheriff Fox and locked up in a holding cell at the town's jail. Shortly after dawn the following morning, Slade was taken from the cell and led before the town judge—Slade's personal friend, Alexander Davis.

Davis was one of the men who had accompanied Slade on his five-month odyssey to bring supplies to Virginia City a year earlier, and he had grown to admire Slade in spite of his rough edges. Several other townsfolk were also in the courtroom, many of them known to be members of the Committee of 100. Among this crowd was X. Beidler and several other vigilantes.

Sheriff Fox began to read the formal charges against Slade. Interestingly, the formal complaint had been signed by the town's madam, Moll Featherlegs. Moll alleged that during the rampage Slade had paid a visit to her bawdyhouse and had partaken liberally of the wares—then not only refused to pay what was owed but shot up the place as well. The veracity of her charges were never substantiated. Although it would not have been unlike many drunken cowboys or ranchers to have visited a bawdyhouse, and certainly not unlike Slade to have shot one up, this is the only recorded instance that suggests Slade ever partook of the offerings of a house of ill repute.

As Sheriff Fox was reading the complaint, Slade appeared to get angrier and angrier. Finally, he literally snatched the paper out of the sheriff's hand, ripped it to shreds, and dropped it onto the floor.

From somewhere—a boot, possibly, or some other hiding place—Slade produced a derringer. Both Beidler and Dimsdale record that Slade stepped forward and pointed the derringer at the head of Judge Davis.

Beidler says Slade, then:

> …sought out Alexander Davis, Judge of the Court, and drawing a cocked derringer, he presented it at his head and told

An artist's depiction of Jack Slade defying the Virginia City court—the "contempt of court" incident that doomed Jack to the hangman's noose. (Courtesy Western History Collection, Denver Public Library)

him that he should hold him as a hostage for his own safety. As the judge stood perfectly quiet and offered no resistance to his captor, no further outrage followed this score.[10]

Sheriff Fox and others in the courtroom stood as if spellbound, and no one moved during this brief Slade soliloquy. Spinning around, Slade released Judge Davis, dropped the derringer into a vest pocket and stormed out of the building. Neither Sheriff Fox nor anyone else in the courtroom made any move to stop him.

X. Beidler followed Slade from the courtroom. Catching up with Slade at the town's feed store, Beidler is said to have told him, "Slade, get on your horse right away and go home or there'll be hell to pay."[11] Another (and more likely) version is that he warned Slade, "get on your horse and get out of town or there'll be hell to pay."

Beidler records no such conversation. Instead, he says that when he caught up with Slade he warned him to get onto his favorite horse, "Copperbottom," and "ride like hell for the border." Slade reacted with a sneer.

"X., it looks like the Vigilante Committee is played out," said Slade, apparently suggesting that because no one tried to stop him at the courtroom, everyone was afraid of him.

"It looks so, but you will change your mind in three hours," responded Beidler—a clear warning to Slade that if he was still available in three hours he would learn just how effective the vigilantes still were.[12]

The quiet statement of Beidler seemed to finally sink in. At last Slade seemed to understand that he was in serious trouble. Apparently deciding the time had come to submit his apologies and offer to pay for the damage, Slade retreated from the store and returned to the courtroom. It was empty.

Notes on Chapter Eleven

1. Some accounts have this lumberyard incident occurring months earlier, before Slade's trip to the Milk River to secure supplies for the area.

2. *X. Beidler: Vigilante*, 97.

3. *The Vigilantes of Montana*, 196.

4. The sixth man, Bill Hunter, escaped but was recaptured and hanged on February 3, 1864. *The Vigilantes of Montana*, 196. See also *The Hanging of Bad Jack Slade*, 37.

5. *Ibid.*, 1. Fairweather struck gold a few weeks later and became one of the wealthiest men in West, if not the world. He spent the money foolishly, however—squandering it on gambling and women, mostly. He died penniless only six years later.

6. *Ibid.*, 38.

7. *The Vigilantes of Montana*, 198.

8. *X. Beidler: Vigilante*, 98.

9. X. Beidler insists the date was March 10, although many other sources give either March 3 or March 4 as the date for this incident.

10. *The Vigilantes of Montana*, 198.

11. Unpublished Manuscript #334, (Denver, CO: Denver Public Library Western History Department), 5.

12. *X. Beidler: Vigilante*, 99.

FINAL CONFRONTATION

ALEXANDER DAVIS was not only a prominent Virginia City citizen and its first judge, he was also an immensely popular man with a reputation for fairness. When Jack Slade grabbed the judge and pointed a derringer at his head, several men slipped out the rear of the courtroom and raced through Alder Gulch spreading the news. The response was instantaneous.

Hundreds of gold miners dropped their picks, grabbed their rifles and began marching toward the courthouse. Dimsdale and Beidler both estimated that six hundred miners came up out of the pits below the city and slowly walked, four abreast, toward the town hall where Slade briefly held the judge prisoner.

Slade must have been aware of this huge demonstration. He was in a serious bind and clearly knew it. His only hope seemed to be for him to find Alexander Davis or other influential local citizens and quickly atone for his sins. Slade walked again from the abandoned courtroom out into the street. There he encountered another old friend and fellow vigilante Dan Harding.

Slade started to apologize to Harding in the pathetic way that men in a panic begin to grovel before anyone who might possibly have some say in the consequences they are about to face. Harding simply held up a hand to silence him.

Speaking in a soft but stern voice, Harding is reported to have told Slade that the Committee had reconsidered its earlier banishment and had now decided to hang him.

Hang him!

Slade took a step backward. Finally he said that only someone like John Lott, a friend of lumberman Langsford, would
try to hang him for such a minor infraction as shooting up the
town. Slade apparently believed that his crime should be considered another childish indiscretion which he could rectify by
simply paying for the damages. He also implied that Lott (or
whoever) surely would not succeed in convincing other vigilantes into compounding the sentence from banishment to
execution. Harding didn't respond.

Slade turned and walked quickly away from Harding. Now
his search for a friend took on a new urgency. Slade strode
quickly along the street, peering into each store he passed.
Eventually his search was rewarded; he found Judge Davis at
the Pfouts & Russell General Store. Perhaps it was not too late.

Slade quickly entered the store and, without preamble,
began to apologize profusely to the judge. He said he was truly
sorry for the spree, explaining that it was the result of his disap-
pointment at being ordered to leave the community he had
grown to love so much. He offered to pay for all damage he
had caused, plus any fine the city cared to impose. While Slade
was speaking, a large crowd of miners, ranchers, and local citizens assembled in front of the store. After a short time several
heavily armed men entered the building.[1]

When Slade noticed the men who had entered the store he
seemed shocked. These were all members of the Committee of
100, but they were not hooded. They stood in a circle around
him, weapons drawn. Outside the store gathered several hundred additional men—those six hundred angry miners,
according to Beidler's estimation. These were "law abiding"
men, along with other citizens of both Virginia City and Nevada City and surrounding territory—men, women and children—who were determined that lawlessness in any form at all
would no longer be tolerated. Especially not lawlessness from
Jack Slade.

Slade's old nemesis Jim Williams was the first to break the silence. Williams stepped from the crowd with a determined look on his face. "Jack Slade," he said solemnly, "the Committee has decided upon your execution."

"My execution?" replied an astounded Slade, who had been expecting banishment, but not death, in spite of the warning moments earlier from Dan Harding. "I've done nothing here to warrant execution! My death? My God, gentlemen, you will not proceed to such extremities!"

Slade, the emotionless killer, the man who had hanged or shot possibly two dozen or more men; Slade the disciplinarian who enforced rules without question and without tolerance for error; this was the Slade who suddenly was reduced to a quivering and pathetic mass of gelatin.

Perhaps his total collapse should not have been surprising. He was neither the first nor the last of the famous tough guys of the frontier who became sniveling cry-babies when faced with the inevitability of their own demise, although Slade had been in tough situations before and handled them quite differently. Maybe he realized that this time his strength and his ability with a six-shooter would not get him out of the jam.

Historian George Hendricks says that men like Jack Slade virtually always collapsed at the end—that is, once they knew death was both imminent and unavoidable:

> The criminal seldom feared law itself; his one great fear was that of being hanged by a body of citizens. Outlaws whose courage and bravery had never before been questioned—men such as Henry Plummer, Hayes Lyons, Dutch John, and Cherokee Bob—broke down completely and wept, crawling on their knees begging vigilantes to spare their lives.[2]

In Slade's case, the collapse was total. Beidler writes, "The doomed man so exhausted himself by tears, prayers, and lamentations, that he had scarcely the strength left to stand under the hangman's beam...."[3]

The remains of the Slade cabin in Montana, the home from which Virginia began her futile dash in an effort to save Jack from a hangman. (Courtesy Western History Collection, Denver Public Library)

A number of other eyewitnesses reported that Slade cried, fell to the floor, and crawled from man to man, begging that he be spared. His appeals went unanswered.

Slade was led (some say "dragged") into a back room at the Pfouts & Russell General Store for a final meeting with the Vigilance Committee. Some accounts say that Slade was given a pencil and paper to write a final note to Virginia, and Beidler says that Slade was permitted one hour to "put his affairs in order." That consisted, apparently, of writing down anything he deemed important. Whether he wrote such a note is uncertain, but all accounts say that during the time allotted to him, he continued to plead for his life.

Newspaperman Dimsdale writes:

> Slade begged to see his wife most piteously, and it seemed hard to deny the request—but the bloody consequences that were sure to follow the inevitable attempt at a rescue that her presence and entreaties would certainly have incited, forbade the granting of his request.[4]

At this moment, a dramatic interruption occurred. One of Slade's ranch hands—possibly one of the men "beaten" by Slade during his drunken rampage the night before—appeared in the store. Speaking of Slade's admirers who now mingled with the hangman's crowd, Dimsdale says, "One of them threw off his coat, and declared that the prisoner could not be hanged until he himself was killed. Promptly, a hundred guns were leveled at him, whereupon he turned and fled."[5]

It was the irony of ironies that in the midst of this grim chain of events, a number of men began to step forward and plead for Jack Slade's life. One spoke of Jack's unselfishness and his courage in saving the community from starvation. Another said that in spite of his rough exterior, Jack Slade was a loyal, trusted friend who consistently went out of his way to help others. A third pleaded that while Jack might be obnoxious, he certainly was not a common horse thief to be hanged by the vigilantes.

Ignoring both Slade and those in the crowd who now were pleading that he be spared, someone in the crowd produced a rope and fashioned a noose in the end. Several men grabbed Slade, and the noose was slipped over his neck. Slade was totally out of control with fear by now—unable to even give the appearance of a courageous or reasonable man.

"My God! My God!," blubbered Slade. "Must I die like this? Oh my poor wife!"[6]

Several men appeared in the room and announced that they had found a suitable place for the hanging—a high crossbeam over a gate at a corral behind and below the Pfouts store.

Citizens of both genders and all ages gathered to watch. A young boy in the crowd who apparently admired Slade slipped away and rode for Virginia Slade. Some say a sympathetic rancher sent the boy on the errand. X. Beidler claims that the vigilantes themselves sent the messenger—after making certain that Slade would be dead long before Virginia could respond.

Whoever made the decision apparently felt that Virginia might be able to successfully plead for his life—or at the least she should know what was going on. Unfortunately for Jack and his wife, the Committee of 100 was in no mood to wait.

Slade was led outside the general store. He was marched straight to the gateway of a corral at the town's livery stable, located on Daylight Creek behind the Pfouts' store—and behind several of the bars Slade had shot up the night before.

A wooden box was placed under the crossbar, and Slade was pushed atop the box. Several men had to brace him to keep him from collapsing. The end of the rope was tossed over the beam. A German immigrant gold miner named Brigham placed the noose around Slade's neck and adjusted it to fit snugly.

At this moment Slade spotted Alexander Davis in the crowd. He appealed to the judge to stop the vigilantes and to become his lawyer. Surprisingly, Davis agreed to do.

Davis made a brief but impassioned appeal for Slade's life. Dimsdale says Davis spoke in a voice so soft that most could not hear his words, but those close enough to understand were moved by his eloquence.

Davis exhorted the crowd not to hang Slade out of frustration over a misdemeanor. He said the Committee members must carefully examine whether they were hanging him for a crime or for his reputation. He reminded the crowd that Slade had saved the town from starvation the previous year and warned that, if they proceeded, they would be known as the only town in history to have hanged a man for contempt of court![8]

At first the crowd nearest the gate was silent while Davis spoke, but it was clear that for the most part they were unmoved by his words. After several minutes the crowd grew restless. Someone in the back shouted, "Hang 'im!" Eventually Davis was drowned out by a chorus of "boos."

Vigilante leader Jim Williams stepped forward and held up his hand for silence. Davis quit talking and stepped back into the crowd. Williams stood squarely in front of Slade and stared him in the eyes. After several seconds of silence Williams said softly but firmly, "Do your duty, boys."

Someone gave Slade a shove, and someone else jerked the box from beneath his feet. Slade twisted and jerked like so many of the men he had hanged. At first he swung wildly back and forth, but gradually the undulations diminished. It was over in a matter of minutes. Slade hung limply in the noose.

Beidler says that although the crowd was adamantly in favor of Slade's hanging, none wanted to appear "ungentlemanly." Vigilante James Kiskadden remarked that it would not be appropriate for Virginia Slade to arrive and find Slade still swinging from the beam, that would be "undignified." Once they were certain he was really dead, Kiskadden, Beidler, and several other men cut down Slade and carried his body to the Virginia City Hotel. They placed him in a rented room, took the ropes off his neck, legs, arms, and feet, and laid him on his back in a "natural repose"—finishing just as Virginia Slade thundered into town on her grey mare.

Mrs. Slade raced up in a cloud of dust and leaped from her horse. She dashed into the hotel and—directed by the pointed hands of onlookers—stumbled into the room reserved for Slade's body. A quick look at her husband told her she was too late.

"You trash!" she shouted. "You hung him like an animal. You could at least have shot him like a man!"

Virginia sobbed for several seconds, then seemed to regain her composure. She rose to her feet and looked again at the men standing around her. "Why, oh, why did not some of you, the friends of Slade, shoot him down and not suffer him to die on the scaffold? I would have done it had I been here. He should never have died by the rope of the hangman. No dog's death should have come to such a man."[7]

The men in the crowd looked a little sheepish. Most stepped backward. Some hung their heads or began quietly slipping away. Virginia continued her harangue as the crowd got smaller and smaller, until at last no one was left to hear her.

Virginia went to the Virginia City undertaker and ordered him to construct a special casket. It was to be zinc-lined[9] in

order to preserve Jack's remains.[10] When the device was completed, Virginia had his body placed into the heavy casket, and
ordered the box to be filled with whiskey and then sealed. She
hoped the alcohol would preserve the remains, which she
planned to take back to Carlyle, Illinois, for burial.

Such a trip was an excruciatingly lengthy one. Because of
continuing trouble with hostile Blackfeet, Lakota and Northern
Cheyenne Indians, the only safe route from Virginia City to
Carlyle passed far southward through Salt Lake City. According
to one account, "…the long coffin rode between the front and
rear boots (of the stagecoach) and produced a sloshing sound as
the coach wheels went over the rough road."[11]

Little is known about that trip. Slade's body apparently was
loaded aboard a Peabody and Caldwell stagecoach for the
rough journey southward. Several weeks passed before Virginia
and her grim cargo arrived at Salt Lake. By then it was apparent to everyone that the zinc-lined casket wasn't effective. Virginia told Salt Lake authorities that the alcohol had not
preserved Jack's body, and that the body of her husband now
smelled so strong she could not continue her journey.

There is little reason to doubt her assertion that the alcohol
preservative was not effective. Salt Lake City records indicate
that Slade was buried on Lot B, Space 67 of the (Salt Lake)
City Cemetery on July 20, 1864. A handwritten note on the
burial document indicated Mrs. Slade planned to have a second coffin constructed, exhume the remains, and eventually
continue the trip eastward.

Her trip was never resumed. It is now known that the
smelly cadaver may not have been the sole reason that Virginia
cut short her husband's last journey at Salt Lake, or the only reason the trip to Illinois was never resumed. There was, in fact,
another and most compelling reason for Virginia to have had a
change of heart about taking Slade back to Carlyle for burial.

Several biographers claim that on the day she arrived in
Salt Lake, the lonely and "grief stricken" widow married one of

the men who had lynched her husband, Montana vigilante James Henry Kiskadden, also known (to Beidler) as Kiscadden. Kiskadden apparently had accompanied Mrs. Slade and her wagon from Virginia City.

Whether Virginia changed her mind about traveling to Illinois specifically because of a new man in her life will never be known. What is known is that Virginia in fact traveled no farther than Salt Lake. It is also a fact that she was seen almost immediately thereafter in Kiskadden's company and married him before much time passed. Whether the couple had been friendly prior to Slade's lynching is unclear, although highly unlikely. It appears more reasonable to assume that the lonely and lovely widow and the strong, handsome vigilante simply took a liking to one another along the lonesome trail between Virginia City and Salt Lake City.

Regardless of when and how they met, Virginia and Mr. Kiskadden didn't remain happy newlyweds for long. They apparently fought almost from the beginning of their marriage and eventually separated. Court records indicate they were divorced less than two years later.

In a strange footnote to the story, Kiskadden then married another woman, a Virginia City saloon entertainer named Annie Adams. In 1872, the marriage produced a daughter born in Salt Lake, who soon joined her mother onstage in a theatrical barnstorming troupe. The daughter, who used the stage name Maude Adams, went on to international theatre fame. She played the lead in the original Broadway production of Peter Pan for several years.[12]

The quiet burial of Jack Slade on July 20, 1864, in Salt Lake's Mormon cemetery was little noted at the time—but it surely should have been. Jack Slade's death, before age thirty-five, ended one of the bloodiest and most interesting sagas in the history of the old West.

Notes on Chapter Twelve

1. Unpublished Manuscript #334, 5.
2. *The Badmen of the West*, 162–3.
3. *The Vigilantes of Montana*, 200.
4. *Ibid.*, 201.
5. *Ibid.*, 201.
6. *Ibid.*
7. *The Hanging of Bad Jack Slade*, 14.
8. *Ibid.*, 5.
9. *An Ear in His Pocket*, 85.
10. Some accounts say the casket was lined with tin.
11. *An Ear in His Pocket*, 85.
12. *Encyclopedia of Frontier Biography*, 837. Some researchers have suggested that the opera star was the daughter of Jack and Virginia Slade, or of Virginia Slade and James Kiskadden. The account given here is correct.

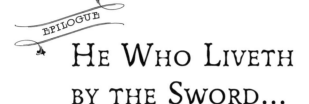
HE WHO LIVETH
BY THE SWORD...

Everything about Jack Slade—from his birth into an educated, sophisticated, moneyed family to his undignified and unheroic death at the hands of vigilantes—was a study in contradictions.

On the one hand was a man who was tough, heartless, cruel, cold-blooded, and emotionless. This was the man who could execute Jules Beni over a twenty-four hour period and seem to enjoy it. It was the man who could coolly execute Indian warriors fighting against Anglo incursion and suspected Wyoming horse thieves with apparent abandon.

On the other hand, Jack Slade was a loving, devoted husband and friend, a loyal employee, a respected boss, a good neighbor, a high achiever, and an apparently thoroughly honest man.

Not surprisingly, his execution by the Montana vigilantes stirred national controversy. Historian C. P. Connolly, a Montana historian and prominent attorney, wrote:

> Slade's execution has been criticized, and no doubt with reason; but one must assuredly conclude that while Slade may not have deserved death, the demands of the hour called imperiously for stern measures.
>
> With the death of Slade, the reign of law (in Montana) began. A peace that had been unknown since the coming of the first gold-seekers settled over the communities of Alder

Gulch. Justice had at least asserted itself, and the rewards of the miner were his own. The curtain had fallen on the first act of the making of the commonwealth.[1]

And indeed the hanging of Slade appeared to mark a significant passing for Montana and the West. It seemed to be a clear watermark; the events that preceded and included it were relics of the lawless, uncivilized, bloody West; the events that succeeded it marked a new, civilized, organized, and much more law-abiding society.

The irony of Jack Slade's death is not that he was hanged; he seemed destined for execution from his childhood years. The enigma is how many people believed Jack Slade was a white knight for law-abiding citizens—that while he may have been flamboyant, he was always honest, loyal, faithful, and honest.

In fact, the German immigrant who placed the noose on Jack Slade's neck, the man named Brigham, later had to flee Montana to avoid retribution by these loyal citizens and followers of Jack Slade.[2]

Some historians are mystified by this reaction to Slade's hanging. They believe that his history of violence alone justified his violent end. Yet even they admit that there were as many who loved him and admired him in death as there were those who believed his hanging ended the era of the badmen. Writing in the years immediately following his death, Thomas Dimsdale wrote:

> Stories of his hanging men and of innumerable assaults, shootings, stabbings, and beatings—in which he was a principal actor—form part of the legends of the stage line; nevertheless, such is the veneration still cherished for him by many of the old stagers that any insult offered to his memory would be fearfully and quickly avenged. Whatever he did to others, he was their friend, they say; and so they will say till the tomb closes over the last of his old friends and comrades of the Overland.[3]

X. Beidler seemed apologetic in the wake of Slade's execution, defending the hanging as a requirement of civilization. Yet Beidler also seemed to recognize that the hanging was simultaneously a great tragedy of the Frontier West:

> The Vigilantes deplored the sad but imperative necessity for making of one example. They acted for the public good, and when examples were made, it was because the safety of the community demanded a warning to the lawless and the desperate, that might neither be despised nor soon forgotten. The execution of the road agents of Plummer's gang was the result of the popular verdict and judgement against robbers and murderers. The death of Slade was the protest of society on behalf of social order and the rights of man.[4]

Newspaperman Dimsdale also seemed apologetic over the hanging, noting that at the time of his death, "(Slade) was never accused or even suspected of either murder or robbery, and the latter crimes were never laid to his charge anyplace else!"[5] As we noted earlier, there were post-execution suggestions that Slade may have been an armed robber or horse thief, but no one made such accusations while he was alive, and no one apparently believed such a possibility during the time Slade roamed the west. No evidence has ever surfaced to connect Slade to such crimes as robbery or cattle rustling or horse stealing.

Judge Alexander Davis is said to have lamented that Jack Slade was not executed for any crime punishable by death, that, in fact, his most serious crime (in Montana) had been to offend the sensitivities of those frontier families that wanted desperately to bring some semblance of society to the great frontier. Davis noted that Slade was condemned to death after insulting Sheriff Fox and the vigilantes who were in the crowd watching the proceedings.

Regardless of whether Slade's hanging was justified, it served its purpose. The hanging sent a message to troublemakers and badmen, giving them reason to think twice before crossing law-abiding citizens on the frontier. Dimsdale was among those who were surprised at the loyalty of Slade's followers. In a newspaper column a few months later, Dimsdale wrote:

> There are probably a thousand individuals in the West possessing a correct knowledge of the leading incidents of a career that terminated at the gallows, who still speak of Slade as a perfect gentleman, and who not only lament his death, but talk in the highest terms of his character, and pronounce his execution a murder![6]

Yet Dimsdale adds that however cruel it may have seemed, and no matter how many people it upset, the execution of Jack Slade had its desired effect:

> The execution of Jack Slade had a most wonderful effect upon society. Henceforth, all knew that no one man could domineer or rule over the community. Reason and civilization then drove brute force from Montana.[7]

It is appropriate that author, newspaperman, and educator Dimsdale write the epitaph for Jack Slade. In his final newspaper column on the activities of the vigilantes, Dimsdale said of Slade:

> Such was Captain J. A. Slade—the idol of his followers, the terror of his enemies and of all that were not within the charmed circle of his dependents. In him, generosity and destructiveness, brutal lawlessness and courteous kindness, firm friendship and volcanic outbreaks of fury.[8]

Notes on Epilogue

1. *True Tales of the West*, 28.
2. Joseph G. Rosa, *The Gunfighters*, 101.
3. *The Vigilantes of Montana*, 204.
4. *Ibid.*, 205.

5. *Ibid.*, 196.
6. *Ibid.*, 195.
7. *Ibid.*, 205.
8. *Ibid.*, 205.

BIBLIOGRAPHY

Writers' Project. Wyoming. *Wyoming; A Guide to its History, Highways and People*. Chicago: Bison Book Edition, 1981.

——. Manuscript #334. Denver: Western History Department, Public Library.

Baaker, Richard S. "Fort Collins (CO) museum notes". Fort Collins Historical Society, 1988.

Beidler, X.X. *Beidler: Vigilante*. Edited by Sanders, Helen Fitzgerald and William H. Bertsche, Jr. Norman, OK: University of Oklahoma Press, 1964.

Billington, Ray Allen. *The Far Western Frontier, 1830–1860*. New York: Harper & Brothers, 1956.

Burrows, William E. *Vigilante*. New York: Harcourt-Brace Company, 1976.

Callaway, Lew. *Montana's Righteous Hangmen: The Vigilantes in Action*. Norman, OK: University of Oklahoma Press, 1982.

Chapman, Arthur. *The Pony Express*. New York: G. P. Putnam's Sons, 1932.

Cody, William F. *The Life of Buffalo Bill*. Hartford, CT: Frank E. Bliss, 1879.

Collins, W. C. *The Hanging of Bad Jack Slade*. Denver, CO: Golden Bell Press, 1963.

Conkling, Roscoe P. and Margaret B. Conkling. *The Butterfield Overland Mail, 1858–1869*. 3 volumes. Glendale, CA: Arthur H. Clark Company, 1947.

Connelly, C.P. *True Tales of the West*. Secaucus, NJ: Castle Publishing, 1985.

Connelley, William E. and Frank A. Root. *The Overland Stage to California*. Topeka, KS: Published by the authors, 1901.

Corbett, Christopher. *Orphans Preferred: The Twisted Truth and Lasting Legend of the Pony Express*. New York: Broadway Books, 2003.

Coutant, C.G. *The History of Wyoming*. Volume 1. New York: Chaplin, Spafford and Mathiessen, 1899.

Di Certo, Joseph J. *The Saga of the Pony Express*. Missoula, MT: Mountain Press Publishing Company, 2002.

Dimsdale, Thomas Josiah. *The Vigilantes of Montana*. Norman, OK: University of Oklahoma Press, 1953.

Ellman, Robert. *Badmen of the West*. London: Hamlyn Publications, 1974.

Fradkin, Philip L. *Stagecoach: Wells Fargo and the American West*. New York: Simon & Schuster, 2002.

Gard, Wayne. *Frontier Justice*. Norman, OK: University of Oklahoma Press, 1949.

Hafen, Le Roy R. *The Overland Mail 1849–1869: Promoter of Settlement Precursor of Railroads*. Cleveland: Aruthur H. Clark Company, 1926.

Hendricks, George D. *The Badmen of the West*. New York: Naylor Company, 1970.

"Illustrating Roughing It." Etext. Mark Twain Archives, University of Virginia. text.lib.virginia.edu/railon/roughingit/illus.

Jackson, W. Turrentine. *Wagon Roads West*. New Haven, CT: Yale University Press, 1965.

Jessen, Kenneth. *Bizarre Colorado: A Legacy of Unusual Events and People*. Loveland, CO: J.V. Publications, 1994.

Jordon, Philip D. *Frontier Law & Order*. Lincoln/London: University of Nebraska Press, 1970.

Lamar, Howard R., ed. *The Readers' Encyclopedia of the American West*. New York: Thomas Y. Crowell Company, 1977.

Matloff, Maurice. *United States Army Historical Series, American Military History*. Washington, DC: Office of the Chief of Military History, United States Army, 1968.

May, Robin. *The Story of the Wild West*. London: Hamlyn Publications, 1978.

Monagham, Jay. *The Book of the American West*. New York: Bonanza Books, 1978.

Moody, Ralph. *Stagecoach West*. New York: Thomas Y. Crowell, 1967.

Nash, Jay Robert. *Bloodletters and Badmen*. New York: Warner Paperback Library, 1975.

Nash, Jay Robert. *Encyclopedia of Western Lawmen and Outlaws.* New York: Paragon House, 1989.

Noyes, Al. *History of Southern Montana.* Helena, MT: State Publishing Company, 1915.

O'Dell, Roy Paul and Kenneth C. Jessen. *An Ear In His Pocket.* Loveland, CO: J.V. Publications, 1996.

O'Neal, Bill. *Encyclopedia of Western Gunfighters.* Norman, OK: University of Oklahoma Press, 1979.

Patterson, Richard M. *Historical Atlas of the Outlaw West.* Boulder, CO: Johnson Books, 1985.

Prassel, Frank Richard. *The Western Peace Officer.* Norman, OK: University of Oklahoma Press, 1972.

Reinfeld, Fred. *Pony Express.* Lincoln-London: University of Nebraska Press, 1973.

Rosa, Joseph G. *They Called Him Wild Bill: The Life and Adventures of James Butler Hickock.* Norman, OK: University of Oklahoma Press, 1964.

Rosa, Joseph G. *The Gunfighters.* Norman, OK: University of Oklahoma Press, 1969.

Scott, Bob. *Blood at Sand Creek.* Caldwell, ID: Caxton Printers, 1994.

Settle, Ramond W. and Mary Lund. *War Drums and Wagon Wheels: The Story of Russell, Majors and Waddell.* Lincoln, NE: University of Nebraska Press, 1966.

Sifakis, Carl. *Encyclopedia of American Crime.* New York: Facts on File, 1973.

Swanson, Evadene Burris. *Fort Collins Yesterdays.* Fort Collins, CO: Don-Art Printers, Inc., 1975.

Thrapp, Dan L. *Encyclopedia of Frontier Biography.* Lincoln/London: University of Nebraska Press, 1988.

Trenholm, Virginia Cole. *Footprints on the Frontier.* Douglas, WY: Douglas Enterprise Company, 1945.

Twain, Mark. *Roughing It.* New York: Viking Press, 1872.

Walker, Henry Pickering. *The Wagonmasters.* Norman, OK: University of Oklahoma Press, 1966.

Watrous, L.L. *History of Larimer County.* New York: Courier Printing and Publishing Company, 1911.

Whitcomb, Elias W. "Reminiscences of a Pioneer." Wyoming State Archives.

Whitcomb, Elias W. Untitled Manuscript. Wyoming State Archives.

Williams, Gerald R. "The Man Who Made Jack Slade Famous." *Colorado Historical Society Magazine*, (May, 1933).

Ubbelhode, Benson & Smith. *A Colorado History*. Boulder, CO: Pruitt Publishing Company, 1982.

Index

About the Author

Bob Scott is a native of Fort Collins, Colorado, near the "heart" of Slade country. He grew up hearing and reading tales about Slade. Nonetheless, his interest in researching and writing about Slade had to take a back seat to other interests for many years. Bob became a radio broadcaster at his hometown station while still in junior high school and went on to pursue a twenty-year career as newscaster in major radio news departments in Denver, Dallas, and Houston. It was during these years that Bob learned to enjoy digging for facts and putting together an understandable and interesting story about often complicated situations. Later, Bob served twenty-five years as station manager and group manager of stations in Colorado, Arizona, Oregon, Texas and Michigan.

His interest in Colorado history first blossomed in 1968 when he learned for the first time of Colorado's important involvement in the U.S. Civil War. Since so little was known about Colorado's role in the war, Bob spent several years researching it and eventually writing his first book on that subject, *Glory, Glory, Glorieta*. The success of that book led to several additional books on frontier America and the Civil War. He always wanted to take time to research and write about Jack Slade and eventually got that opportunity beginning in 1993, research that eventually led to this book.

He is an accomplished commercial/instrument pilot with 10,000 hours piloting time, and a much in-demand speaker at colleges, historical societies, and other gatherings. His biography is included in *Who's Who in Aviation and Aerospace (1983)* and the *Who's Who National Registry (1998)*. He describes himself as a great hunter, an average fisherman, and a lousy golfer.

Bob is married to Heather Ann Letcavage, and is the father of two daughters, three sons, and two grandsons. Now semi-retired and living in central Pennsylvania, he is currently working on two additional books dealing with colorful characters and events in American history.

Notes on the production of this book

This book was printed simultaneously in two editions.

A *special limited hardcover edition* of only 400 copies was Symth sewn and bound in Tudor Brown Skiver Kivar 7, embossed with Coach gold foil, and wrapped in a four-color dustjacket.

The special edition contains a High Plains Press limited edition bookplate, designed and hand-printed from a woodcut on Mohawk Superfine archival paper by Richard Wagener. Each bookplate is individually signed by the author and hand-numbered.

A *softcover trade edition* was issued simultaneously. It is covered with twelve-point stock, printed in four colors, and coated with a special matte finish.

The text of all editions is composed in twelve-point Adobe Garamond. Display type is Oldbook ITC, Henderson Bold and Kick ITC

The book is printed on fifty-five pound EB Natural paper by Edwards Brothers.